The Z Factor

Transforming Business for the Next Generation

by
Alex Sterling

The Z Factor

Transforming Business for the Next Generation

Contents

Introduction

In the fast-paced and continuously evolving business landscape, a new cohort has emerged with the potential to reshape the very fabric of how we work, communicate, and innovate. This is Generation Z – a group of young, vibrant individuals who have never known a world without the internet, social media, and a global connection at their fingertips. As they step into the workforce, they bring with them a fresh perspective and a digital dexterity that can no longer be viewed as merely advantageous but essential for organisations aiming to thrive in the modern era.

The incorporation of Generation Z into the workplace is not without its challenges, but therein also lies unprecedented opportunities. These emerging professionals are hardwired for the digital age, with insights and skills that can drive innovation and create a dynamic, inclusive, and future-ready business environment. Forward-thinking executives, HR leaders, and organisational strategists can benefit immensely by understanding how to leverage the inherent abilities of this generation to foster growth and competitiveness.

This book is designed as a comprehensive guide, providing the knowledge and tools necessary to effectively integrate Generation Z into the workforce. It aims to enhance not just innovation and inclusivity, but also sustainability within the modern business landscape. The goal is to empower you to harness the potential of Gen Z's unique characteristics, blending their fresh perspectives with the experience of preceding generations to forge a powerful collective force.

As we delve further into these pages, we shall explore the distinguishing attributes of Generation Z: their relentless pursuit of innovation, their innate entrepreneurial spirit, and their unwavering commitment to sustainability and social responsibility. We'll examine how these qualities can be harnessed to not only revolutionise work practices but also to cultivate a robust corporate culture that resonates with young workers today.

The advent of this new workforce heralds a significant shift in technological prowess. Gen Z's fluency in disruptive technologies such as artificial intelligence, virtual reality, and cybersecurity is set to redefine the boundaries of what's possible in the workplace. Understanding how to align these skills with business objectives is crucial for staying ahead of the curve.

Furthermore, this book will guide you through the paradigms of leadership and engagement that resonate with Gen Z. New approaches to communication, training, and development will be unveiled, recognising the need for more tailored, flexible, and collaborative strategies. These are essential in cultivating a work environment where every employee, regardless of generational affiliation, can thrive and contribute to the overall mission of the business.

Gen Z's entry into the workforce also calls for innovative recruitment strategies and workspace design, both of which are critical in attracting and retaining young talent. We'll explore how balancing physical office spaces with flexible remote work arrangements can create the agile environments needed for these digital natives to flourish. Effective communication techniques, leveraging social media and digital platforms, are just as important in building bridges with Gen Z candidates and employees.

Even the most seasoned leaders may find themselves needing to adapt and evolve their approaches to match the changing expectations of this new generation. Leadership development, succession planning, and crafting inclusive, forward-looking workplace cultures are going to be key components in the integration process. It's about understanding Gen Z's worldview and aligning it with the organisation's values and objectives.

A crucial aspect of engaging with Gen Z is developing a robust understanding of their financial goals and compensation expectations. Aligning rewards with their aspirational goals without overlooking the diversity and inclusivity that are core to their identity is paramount for success.

Moving further, we will unpack the significance of health and wellbeing for Gen Z workers, acknowledging their preference for work-life integration over balance and the increasing importance of mental health and emotional intelligence in the workplace. In a world where business practices are scrutinised for their ethical implications, we will also reflect on how corporate social responsibility initiatives resonate with the Gen Z ethos, fostering loyalty and a sense of empowerment.

As the legal landscape continues to evolve alongside technological advancements and the introduction of new work paradigms, this book will touch upon the relevant legal considerations and compliance issues that pertain to including Gen Z in the workforce. Navigating employment law and data protection will be critical factors for maintaining harmony and integrity within organisational structures.

Lastly, we must prepare not only for the immediate future but for the continuous evolution of the workplace. Peering beyond Gen Z, we situate ourselves at the cusp of welcoming the Alpha Generation, signalling the importance of lifelong learning and ongoing adaptation as cornerstones of sustainable business practices.

With each chapter, this book will build upon the foundation laid in this introduction, creating not just a blueprint for integrating Gen Z into the workplace but an actionable strategy that can be custom-tailored to fit the unique context of your business. In doing so, our collective journey will not only capture the essence of Gen Z but also sculpt the very future of work itself.

Chapter 1:
The Emergence of Generation Z

In the evolving tapestry of the workforce, a new pattern has emerged with the arrival of Generation Z. Born into a world where the rapid advancement of technology has redefined life's every aspect, this cohort brings a unique blend of resourcefulness, digital fluency, and a socially conscious ethos to the professional arena. As they step into adulthood and permeate corporate corridors, their entrance marks a bold transition, catalysing fundamental shifts in workplace culture. For leaders, the realisation that a fresh perspective has docked at their shores presents an opportunity—not just to question existing paradigms but to actively embrace the change. Grasping the Z factor isn't just about acknowledging their numerative strength; it's about recognising the intricate weave of their character, aspirations, and the innovative spirit that they harbour. It's time for organisations to dive deep into understanding the defining characteristics of Gen Z, bridging generational divides and capitalising on the dynamic transformation this generation can ignite in the pursuit of a thriving, future-ready business environment.

Understanding the Z Factor

As we delve into the heart of the 'Emergence of Generation Z', it's crucial to grasp the 'Z Factor', a unique blend of characteristics and imperatives that set this generation apart in the workspace. Generation Z isn't just another demographic cohort to mould into existing frameworks; they are catalysts for profound transformation. They're digital dynamos, with an intrinsic grasp of technology that underpins their approach to work and life. Their worldview is decidedly global, attitudes towards diversity and inclusion are staunchly progressive, and their quest for purpose aligns with an indomitable entrepreneurial streak. Decoding the essence of the Z Factor isn't merely academic; it's the cornerstone for businesses aiming to harness the fresh perspectives and innovative potential that these young professionals bring to the table. Therefore, to capitalise on this generational shift, organisations must align their strategic vision with the proclivities and paradigms of Gen Z, creating an environment where this next wave of talent doesn't just survive but thrives, driving growth in an increasingly complex and interconnected marketplace.

The Defining Characteristics of Gen Z

We've established the backdrop against which Generation Z is coming of age, their nuanced view of the world forged by the unique historical, social, and technological landscapes they have navigated. Now, as organisational strategists, it's imperative to dive deeper into this demographic's defining characteristics to better adapt and reap the benefits of their inclusion in today's workforce.

Foremost, Gen Zers have been born into a digital ecosystem. Unlike previous generations, they don't know a world without smartphones, social media, or instant access to information. This digital fluency means they're not just comfortable with technology—they expect it to permeate all aspects of their lives, including the workplace. Utilising this tech-savviness can lead to dramatic strides in efficiency and creativity.

Another core trait of this generation is their entrepreneurial mindset. Many have seen the pitfalls of traditional employment paths through the experiences of older peers and have consequently adopted a 'do-it-yourself' attitude. Organisations that nurture this spirit within their cultures can unearth a wealth of innovative thinking.

Gen Zers tend to be more pragmatic and financially minded than their Millennial predecessors, partly due to witnessing the economic turbulence of the late 2000s. This financially astute generation is likely to value stability and are drawn to employers who can provide it, as well as those who are transparent about growth and income prospects.

The youngest working generation places a strong emphasis on individuality and authenticity, both in how they present themselves and in their expectations from brands and employers. They want to work for companies that aren't just providing lip service to values, but are actively demonstrating a commitment to ethical practices. This is a cohort that is willing to stand up for what they believe is right, and they respect leaders who do the same.

A key attribute of Gen Z is their commitment to social and environmental issues. They want to make a difference in the world, and they seek out employers that align with their desire for social impact. For businesses, this means that sustainability and CSR initiatives aren't just nice to have—they're crucial for attracting and retaining Gen Z talent.

A diverse and inclusive workplace isn't optional for Gen Z; it's expected. Having grown up in a more connected and globalised society, they place a high value on diversity of thought, background, and experience. In response, businesses must ensure that their recruitment and retention strategies genuinely reflect these values.

Their communication style leans towards the direct and visual. Accustomed to swiftly absorbing information via platforms like Instagram and YouTube, Gen Zers prefer modes of communication that are straightforward and media-rich over lengthy emails or documents. Adapting corporate communication to be more succinct and visually engaging can greatly enhance understanding and engagement.

This generation seeks feedback and recognition, but not in the traditional sense of annual reviews. Instead, they favour regular, real-time feedback that allows them to continually adjust and develop. For organisations, this could mean a transformation in performance management systems towards more dynamic, ongoing mentoring and support frameworks.

Work-life balance for Gen Z translates to work-life integration. They've grown up multitasking across devices and see no reason why their careers shouldn't be equally fluid and flexible. Today's businesses must offer and encourage styles of working that allow for a blending of personal and professional life.

Mental health awareness is significantly more pronounced amongst Gen Zers, who are generally more open about discussing these issues and expect their employers to support their wellbeing. This means that wellness programs and supportive policies are not just a perk, but a key element of an organisation's value proposition to attract this generation.

Customised career paths also resonate with this generation's desire for personalisation. Gen Z workers are looking for opportunities to build a career that reflects their strengths and interests and will gravitate towards organisations that provide the resources to chart such paths.

Furthermore, due to their inherent grasp of global connectivity, Gen Zers are proficient at working across cultural boundaries and expect multicultural perspectives to be appreciated and incorporated into the business strategy. For organisations, this presents a valuable resource for driving innovation in an increasingly global marketplace.

What sets this generation apart, too, is their view of success. The emphasis has shifted from the singular pursuit of financial gain to a broader definition that includes personal fulfilment and impactful work. Businesses that communicate and embody a vision that transcends profits will resonate more deeply with Gen Z professionals.

In learning the defining characteristics of Gen Z, organisations are provided with a blueprint for fostering environments that not only attract but also inspire this capable generation. Through understanding and embracing their distinct attitudes towards technology, entrepreneurship, diversity, communication, work-life balance, mental health, and social responsibility, businesses can unlock a dynamic and inclusive workplace ready for present challenges and future advancements.

Bridging the Generational Divide

In this dynamic era dominated by Generation Z's entrance into the workforce, an organisational imperative stands out: to bridge the generational divide. It's essential to acknowledge the multifaceted mosaic of values, aspirations, and work styles that each generation brings to the table. By nurturing an environment that leverages the tech-savvy and progressive mindset of Gen Z while dovetailing it with the experience and resilience of older generations, creative synthesis can emerge. Businesses must champion intergenerational mentorship programmes and create spaces for knowledge exchange that defy the traditional top-down flow. There's a wealth of opportunity in empowering Gen Z to be trailblazers while still drawing on the wisdom of their predecessors. Only by harmonising the strengths across generations can organisations truly tap into a wellspring of innovation that drives business forward and crafts a resilient, future-proof work culture.

The Impact on Workplace Dynamics

The integration of Generation Z into today's businesses stands as a turning point in the evolution of workplace dynamics. With each new generation, there comes an influx of fresh perspectives, behaviours, and preferences - and Gen Z is no exception. While their predecessors have already established legacies of their own, the youngest cohort in the workforce is redefining what collaboration, communication, and career development should look like in a modern setting.

Foremost, Gen Z's entrance into the marketplace has starkly highlighted the necessity for technology at the core of business operations. Their aptitude for digital platforms means that they're not just equipped to use technology; they expect it to be threaded through every facet of their workday. Consequently, organisations that wish to harness the full potential of these young minds must ensure their technological infrastructures are not only current but also agile enough to adapt to rapid advancements.

The mindset of Gen Z also encompasses a drive for autonomy and personal growth. Raised in an era where personal branding and online businesses have flourished, they aspire to work within environments that celebrate individual ingenuity. Managers and team leaders are thus finding themselves grappling with how to provide structured guidance while granting the autonomy Gen Z craves. This dance between freedom and direction is recalibrating leadership styles and team dynamics in considerable ways.

Fuelled by an unprecedented access to global information, Gen Z employees often manifest an intrinsic social consciousness that influences their work ethic. Expectations for their employers to not only turn a profit but also contribute to social causes have birthed a wave of corporate social responsibility initiatives. The talent of tomorrow is looking to work for companies that stand for something beyond their business objectives, thus putting pressure on organisations to align with ethical practices and sustainability.

Communication is another facet of workplace dynamics that is undergoing transformation. Gen Z favours succinct, clear, and instantaneous exchanges, often facilitated by the latest apps and software. Their preference for engaging visuals and bite-sized content is reshaping corporate communications, with an increasing shift towards video and interactive media over long-form emails and documents. This shift demands existing employees and management to adapt quickly to maintain effective collaboration.

The importance placed by Gen Z on work-life integration rather than work-life balance encourages businesses to consider more than just the number of hours worked. They're pushing for an approach that favours productive, purposeful work that allows them ample time for personal pursuits and wellbeing. Companies are thus tasked with rethinking job roles, flexible scheduling, and even reassessing the traditional 9-to-5 workday.

Gen Z's presence in the workforce has acted as a catalyst for a greater push towards inclusivity and diversity. Organisations are recognising the necessity to not just include a variety of perspectives for compliance's sake, but to imbibe them as integral contributors to innovation and problem-solving. A diverse workforce can no longer be a check-the-box initiative; it must be a living, breathing aspect of company culture to attract and retain Gen Z talent.

Mentorship programs have seen a resurgence, with a shift from a top-down approach to a more collaborative exchange of knowledge and skills. The lines between mentor and mentee are often blurred with Gen Z, where the learning is mutual and reciprocal. Companies investing in these programs find they not only aid in personal development but also serve as a bridge between different generational cohorts within the workplace.

Recognition and feedback mechanisms are undergoing a significant overhaul in response to Gen Z's expectations. Annual performance reviews are giving way to more frequent, informal, and real-time feedback sessions. Organisations are crafting gamified reward systems and continuous feedback platforms to meet the need for instantaneous, constructive, and public recognition that Gen Zers are accustomed to in their digital lives.

It's becoming increasingly clear that trust is a crucial element for Gen Z. They prefer transparent management and clear articulation of company goals and challenges. A lack of transparency can undermine their trust in leadership and diminish their engagement. This need is fostering an era where open communication policies and transparent decision-making processes are becoming the norm in proactive organisations.

Learning and development is another arena where the impact of Gen Z is markedly felt. They're lifelong learners by nature; thus, the traditional model of intensive upfront training followed by sporadic updates is falling out of favour. Instead, a continuous learning approach where microlearning, online platforms, and self-directed education dominate is more appealing to Gen Z professionals who value constant evolution over stagnant skill sets.

As digital natives, Gen Z employees bring a fresh perspective on data security and the role of privacy in the workplace. They are acutely aware of the value of their personal data and expect their employers to be rigorous about cybersecurity. This consciousness around digital privacy is prompting organisations to ramp up their security measures and educate their workforce about data protection best practices.

The necessity for organisational agility has never been more pronounced. In a world where Gen Z can rapidly shift from one trend or tool to the next, companies are compelled to be as dynamic as their youngest employees. Traditional hierarchies are being challenged to evolve into more fluid and adaptable structures capable of responding swiftly to change.

Lastly, the concept of career progression is being reinvented. Gen Z often approaches their careers as a series of experiences rather than a ladder to climb. This has significant implications for how career paths are structured, and opportunities are offered within organisations. A more modular, flexible approach to career development that allows for lateral moves, skill acquisition, and role variations suits the Gen Z's appetite for variety and challenge.

In conclusion, Generation Z's entry into the workforce is more than a mere generational handover; it's a transformative juncture that is reshaping workplace dynamics on multiple fronts. To stay ahead, forward-thinking executives and HR leaders must strive to understand and harness the unique attributes of this cohort, thereby creating a thriving environment for all in the modern business landscape.

Chapter 2:
Gen Z: A Portrait

As we delve further into the idiosyncrasies of Generation Z, it's imperative to paint a vivid portrait of these young individuals storming into the professional sphere with a digital-first mentality. Gen Zers, having been weaned on the internet and social platforms, are not just comfortable with technology—they are its native inhabitants, poised to navigate and reshape the future of work with ease and innovation. Their upbringing in a world teeming with global challenges has also imbued them with a set of core values and work expectations that starkly differentiate them from predecessors. Their desire for authenticity, inclusivity, and purpose in their careers is not just a preference but a demand. Understanding Gen Z requires a nuanced appreciation of their holistic worldview where work, personal identity, and social consciousness are inextricably linked—an understanding that paves the way for their seamless integration into workplaces intent on being at the forefront of progress.

Digital Natives in a Changing World

As we delve into the heart of what defines Generation Z, it's essential to comprehend the profound impact of their digital nativity. Born into a world where the internet is a fundamental aspect of daily life, Gen Z's connection with digital technology is intrinsic to their identity. They manoeuvre the online realm with an ease that previous generations simply can't rival. This pervasive digital environment has significantly altered the landscape in which they grow, socialise, and, crucially, will ultimately work.

The ramifications of their digital fluency reach far beyond familiarity with the latest apps or social media trends. For Gen Z, digital technology is not merely a tool; it is an extension of their consciousness and an integral component of their thought process. As a result, they perceive and engage with the world in ways that are distinctively different from their predecessors. This generation is uniquely equipped to navigate a labyrinth of online information, to discern innovative solutions from an early age, and to adapt rapidly to technological shifts.

With continual exposure to global conversations and limitless data, Gen Z's worldview is expansive. They are less restricted by geographical boundaries and more cognisant of international issues and diverse perspectives. Their access to an array of viewpoints fosters a culture where adaptability and continuous learning are paramount. In their eyes, skills can always be honed, knowledge always expanded, and nothing is ever static—sentiments that resonate with the very nature of the digital age.

However, this digital prowess comes with its own set of challenges. Gen Z enters the workforce at a critical juncture, where digital transformation is disrupting traditional business models. They expect workplaces to mirror the digital sophistication they have become accustomed to. This includes leveraging advanced communication tools, adopting flexible remote work policies, and cultivating workplaces that support rapid innovation and collaboration.

Business leaders must recognise the digital-first mindset of Gen Z and its potential to revolutionise workplace norms. Traditional hierarchical structures are less appealing to this cohort; they thrive in environments that favour a flat organisational culture, where ideas can be shared freely and everyone is heard, irrespective of their position.

This shift in dynamic can lead to a more democratized workplace where contributions from all levels are valued. It's a breeding ground for innovation that older generations might find unorthodox yet is second nature to digital natives.

Their ease with technology also implies that Gen Z values efficiency and expects results at a pace that matches their digital experiences. They are accustomed to the instantaneity of information retrieval and communication and anticipate a similar responsiveness from their work environments. Consequently, workplaces need to accelerate their process flows and eradicate any unnecessary bureaucratic hurdles to maintain pace with Gen Z's expectations.

Gen Z's digital immersion has heightened their awareness of cybersecurity risks. They seek assurance that their data, and by extension, their privacy, is safeguarded. Organisations must not only ensure robust cybersecurity frameworks but also transparently communicate these measures to alleviate Gen Z's concerns. This is a fundamental step in building trust and a sense of security among Gen Z employees.

Moreover, Gen Z's propensity for digital consumption means they value content that is succinct, visually engaging, and easily digestible. When it comes to corporate training and development, microlearning modules and interactive, gamified experiences are more effective in capturing their attention and fostering retention. It's this type of innovation in educational delivery that will engage and develop the Gen Z workforce.

One of the most profound traits of Gen Z is their entrepreneurial spirit, which is amplified by digital platforms that offer unprecedented access to markets and resources. They are inclined to take initiative and value employers that provide autonomy and opportunities to contribute meaningfully. Businesses that can harness this entrepreneurial drive stand to benefit from a workforce that is inherently focused on growth and continuous improvement.

Additionally, the amplified use of social media has armed Gen Z with a robust sense of community and collective action. They're not merely content with doing a job; they want to be part of a cause that aligns with their values. Organisations that champion social responsibility, inclusivity, and transparency will resonate deeply with this generation. It's not just about the work anymore—it's about the impact of that work on the wider world.

As the digitization of society accelerates, Gen Z's inherent abilities position them uniquely as catalysts for change in the workplace. Businesses need to catch up with their pace, utilise their skills to the fullest and harness their innovative potential. In turn, Gen Z offers a chance to elevate standard practices, integrate progressive thinking, and drive forward a new era of corporate evolution.

At the same time, organisations should be mindful of not just leveraging Gen Z's skills but also fostering their growth. This means creating spaces that encourage critical thinking, problem-solving, and leadership. It involves providing resources for continuous learning and platforms for their voices to be heard. Such investment in Gen Z's potential is not just favourable but essential for any forward-thinking business.

In essence, as digital natives in a changing world, Gen Z represents the advent of a new paradigm in the workforce. Their expectations are reshaping the corporate landscape, compelling organisations to adapt to their digital-first, agile, and value-driven ethos. For businesses, this is a clarion call to reevaluate and modernise their cultures, strategies, and infrastructures to align with the future now embodied by Gen Z.

Understanding and integrating Generation Z into the workforce signals a sea change in the way businesses operate, innovate, and compete. It's a change characterised by digital fluency, cultural agility, and a relentless pursuit of purpose. In recognising the exceptional capacities and desires of Gen Z, organisations can anticipate their needs, catalyse innovation, and pave the way for a dynamic, inclusive, and future-ready business environment.

Values and Expectations of the New Workforce

As the baton of innovation and work ethic is passed to Generation Z, understanding their core values and expectations is paramount for any organisation seeking longevity and relevance in tomorrow's market. This rising demographic enters the workforce with a unique blend of characteristics influenced by socio-economic changes, technological advancements, and global connectivity.

One of the pivotal values that define Gen Z is their demand for authenticity and transparency. They've grown up amidst a digital revolution, where information is at their fingertips. They expect the same level of openness from their employers, whether that's company's financial health or its ethical practices. Leadership cannot afford to hide behind corporate veils; honesty is not just preferred, it's expected.

Diversity and inclusivity are not just HR buzzwords for Gen Z; they're non-negotiable standards for their employers. With the world's rich tapestry of cultures made accessible through social platforms, they've cultivated an inclusive mindset. For them, a diverse workforce fosters creativity and innovation. Companies lacking in this area will struggle to attract and retain young talent.

The discussion on work-life balance has shifted dramatically with Generation Z. They seek integration, not simply a balance. Flexible work hours, remote working options, and a focus on mental health are high on their list of priorities. They desire careers that accommodate their life choices, rather than dictating them, reflecting a holistic approach to employment.

Linked closely to their life integration philosophy is the aspect of mental health. Gen Z is more open about discussing mental health than any previous generation, and they expect their workplace to support their psychological well-being. Businesses will find that investing in this area is not just ethically sound, but it also pays dividends in terms of productivity and employee retention.

Undoubtedly, Gen Z is reshaping the concept of loyalty within the workplace. They're loyal to causes, to ethical practices, and to personal growth opportunities rather than to brands or companies alone. As such, career progression and continuous learning are essential. The prospect of upskilling and expanding their knowledge base is a powerful incentive for them to join and stay with a company.

The central role of technology in the lives of Gen Z cannot be overstated. Digital literacy is an intrinsic part of their identity—they expect their employers to be technologically savvy as well. The implementation of advanced tech and digital tools is a barometer for a company's commitment to staying at the industry's cutting edge in the eyes of Gen Z.

Sustainability is another cornerstone. This generation has inherited significant environmental challenges and holds both themselves and their employers to high standards when it comes to ecological preservation. Corporate social responsibility and eco-friendly policies are not only appreciated but also anticipated by Gen Z.

Gen Z's entrepreneurial spirit translates into expectations for a dynamic and agile work environment. They thrive in workplaces that stimulate innovation and allow them autonomy in their projects. Organisations with rigid structures and hierarchies will have to evolve to serve the creativity and independent thought that this generation brings to the table.

Financial security and competitive remuneration packages are crucial, but they're viewed differently by Gen Z. They see compensation as multifaceted—it includes salary, yes, but also benefits like health care, professional development funds and other non-traditional forms of compensation like stock options or profit-sharing.

Our ascending cohort is also focused on impact. They want to work for companies making a positive difference in the world. They aren't afraid to hold their employers accountable, often evaluating their roles and responsibilities through the lens of social impact. An employer's legacy is important, but even more so is their active role in crafting a better future.

Feedback and a collaborative atmosphere rank high among Gen Z's workplace must-haves. They eschew traditional annual reviews in favour of continuous, constructive and real-time feedback mechanisms. It's part of a broader expectation for a communicative workplace culture where ideas flow freely and improvements are iterative rather than episodic.

Privacy and cyber security are critical to this cohort, and they expect their employers to be staunch defenders of data protection. This generation, having grown up amidst numerous high-profile data breaches and an increasing awareness of digital surveillance, require peace of mind that their personal information is safe and secure.

Lastly, leadership to Gen Z means a combination of mentorship, inspiration, and facilitation. They look for leaders who can guide without micromanaging, who can provoke thought without imposing views, and who can create a pathway for success within the organisation, allowing Gen Z employees to not just grow but to flourish.

Their values and expectations paint a picture of a workforce that is multi-dimensional, socially conscious, and tech-enabled. As such, the successful integration of Gen Z in the workplace demands companies stay nimble, progressive, and genuine. It's a tall order, but for businesses that can adapt, the rewards—a dedicated, innovative, and transformative workforce—are limitless.

Chapter 3:
The Gen Z Mindset

Building on the comprehensive profile of Generation Z sketched out in the previous chapter, let's delve into the Gen Z mindset—a rich tapestry of innovation, entrepreneurship, sustainability, and social responsibility. Gen Z are not merely employees; they stand as the vanguard of a seismic shift in the corporate world. Equipped with a digital-first approach, they meld their native tech fluency with a bold, entrepreneurial streak, pushing boundaries and challenging the status quo. At the same time, their keen sense of global citizenship calls for meaningful work that aligns with their deep-seated ethical convictions. For the forward-thinking executive, understanding the Gen Z mindset isn't simply about bridging a generational gap—it's a vital step towards crafting a vibrant, inclusive, and progressive workplace culture that's responsive to the zeitgeist of the 21st century and beyond.

Innovation and Entrepreneurial Spirit

The essence of the Generation Z mindset can't be captured in a singular dimension, yet two facets shimmer distinctively: innovation and entrepreneurial spirit. As we delve deeper into the intricacies of what drives this cohort, it becomes evident that these inherent characteristics not only define them but are also reshaping our workplaces and business practices. We must carefully analyse and adapt to these traits if we aim to harness Gen Z's full potential within the workforce.

Gen Zers have been touted as the most entrepreneurial generation to date. This stems in part from their immersion in a digital world where platforms enable them to launch start-ups from their bedrooms. They've witnessed young entrepreneurs scale businesses rapidly through technology and are inspired to follow suit. They're bold, they're driven, and they often seek to carve out their own paths over climbing traditional corporate ladders.

This entrepreneurial inclination translates into a mindset that values flexibility, creativity, and autonomy—traits that are not just useful but essential for innovation. Thus, integrating Gen Z into our current business environment means fostering these qualities, allowing this generation to explore and push boundaries at the workplace just as they would in their personal ventures.

Yet, their entrepreneurial spirit doesn't signify a disdain for collaboration. On the contrary, they thrive in dynamic, team-oriented settings where ideas can cross-pollinate. They're tuned into the power of crowdsourcing and understand that a collective can often innovate more effectively than the individual. Companies that create environments mirroring the openness and inclusivity of online communities may find themselves at the forefront of innovation.

Moreover, Gen Z's approach to innovation is iterative and agile. Raised in a world of constant updates and rapid iterations, they're comfortable with the idea that a product or service can go to market before it's 'perfect' and improve over time. This mindset can lead to a paradigm shift in how we develop business models, allowing for greater adaptability and responsiveness to market demands.

For organizations, leveraging Gen Z's innovative capabilities means embracing a culture that permits calculated risk-taking and rewards ingenuity. In practice, this could mean instituting policies that allow for 'fail fast, learn fast' approaches or setting up creative labs where young employees can experiment with new ideas without the fear of repercussion.

Data-driven decision-making is second nature to Gen Z. They've grown up with advanced analytics and expect to leverage data in creative and meaningful ways. Companies that provide access to data and tools will empower these young innovators to identify patterns and insights, leading to informed experimentation and strategic business solutions.

It's crucial to acknowledge that innovation isn't confined to products—it's equally important in processes. Gen Zers are not tethered to legacy systems; they are looking to improve efficiency and productivity through novel solutions. Executives must be open to overhauling outdated practices, as this generation might hold the key to streamlining operations that have been status quo for decades.

The connection between Gen Z and technological innovation is unmistakable. They have an intuitive grasp of digital tools that can streamline communication, automate mundane tasks, and create new channels for service delivery. Their natural propensity for tech means they are well-equipped to lead the charge in digital transformation initiatives within companies.

But it's not just about tech savviness. Gen Z is also deeply motivated by purpose and impact. For them, innovation is meaningful only if it contributes positively to society. They're keen on initiating projects that have the potential to address social issues, echoing the need for businesses to be purpose-driven. Their ideas often encapsulate social entrepreneurship, combining profit with societal benefits.

Peer-to-peer learning is ingrained in the Gen Z culture. They look for reciprocative environments where they can share their skills and learn from others. In such an atmosphere, idea-sharing becomes organic and almost reflexive, leading to a continual flow of innovation.

Modern businesses must structure their teams to capitalize on this collaborative learning spirit.

Gen Z's penchant for disruption extends to the traditional employer-employee relationship. They are not satisfied with being mere cogs in the machine; they want a seat at the table, a voice in decision-making, and a stake in the entrepreneurial game. They pursue work environments where their opinions and ideas are valued, and where they feel they can make a tangible difference.

However, embedding a culture of innovation in an organisation isn't without its challenges. It necessitates a shift from top-down hierarchy to a more lateral structure where ideas can germinate at all levels. Unlocking this within an existing corporate setup demands visionary leadership and a commitment to long-term cultural change.

Finally, to truly benefit from the Gen Z drive for innovation, companies must align their incentive systems appropriately. This generation is motivated by progression and personal growth. Offering pathways for rapid advancement and recognising achievements innovatively can encourage Gen Z to fully invest their talents in a company's mission.

In conclusion, the innovation and entrepreneurial spirit of Generation Z is not just a footnote in the annals of workforce evolution; it's a powerful force that can redefine how we approach business, technology, and societal challenges. It's imperative for forward-thinking executives and HR leaders to not just accommodate but actively nurture this spirit within their organisational strategies to create a dynamic, inclusive, and robust business environment for the future.

Sustainability and Social Responsibility

In the fabric of contemporary business strategies, sustainability and social responsibility are interwoven threads pivotal to understanding the Gen Z mindset. This cohort brings an acute consciousness of the global issues that face their generation, including environmental degradation, climate change, and social inequities. They're not merely content with observing; they want to be active participants in crafting a brighter, more sustainable future.

The conversation about sustainability is no longer periphery for corporations; it's a core concern. Gen Z employees are pushing companies to move beyond token gestures and embed genuine, impactful sustainability practices into their business models. They are the generation of 'prosumers', being both producers and consumers who advocate for and align with brands that prioritize ethical environmental policies.

Corporate social responsibility (CSR) has had to evolve radically to meet Gen Z's expectations. Companies must now demonstrate a deep commitment to the social issues that resonate with this generation, from championing diversity and inclusion to ensuring fair trade practices and human rights are upheld in every corner of their supply chains.

One element that stands out in Gen Z's approach is their unwavering demand for transparency. They expect brands not just to claim they are green and socially responsible, but also to prove it with data and actions that show ongoing improvement. This generation's influence is reflected in the growing prevalence of sustainability reports and third-party validations in the corporate world.

However, while Gen Z's idealism is commendable, it must also be integrated in a balanced manner within the current market structures. It's not merely about overhauling systems overnight but progressively steering them towards greater corporate citizenship. Businesses that heed this balance find themselves attracting and retaining Gen Z talent more effectively.

Active engagement in sustainability also presents an innovative frontier. These younger workers are valuable assets in ideating and implementing green initiatives, from waste reduction and energy-efficient processes to developing sustainable products and services. Their digital fluency, moreover, aligns seamlessly with the Internet of Things (IoT) and green tech solutions, hinting at how deeply they can influence sustainable innovation.

It's essential to note that Gen Z's focus on social responsibility extends beyond environmental concerns. They are ardent supporters of philanthropy and volunteering, often seeking out employers that facilitate opportunities for giving back to the community. This is a stark reflection of their desire to work for organisations that don't exist solely for profit but also contribute positively to society.

On the front of social entrepreneurship, this generation is propelling a shift towards businesses that can solve societal issues and generate revenue simultaneously. The traditional not-for-profit sector, in their view, should intersect more strategically with business ventures, each complementing the other to engender holistic societal impact.

The implication for leaders and strategists is distinct: aligning with Gen Z's sustainability and social responsibility ethos means enacting and upholding principles that underpin their conceptualisation of ethical business. It's about building companies that deliver value not just to shareholders, but to stakeholders at large—which includes the planet and its diverse inhabitants.

There is also a pressing need for corporate leaders to communicate their sustainability and social responsibility initiatives effectively. Gen

Z yearns for authentic narratives that showcase an organisation's earnest efforts and real-world impacts, rather than superficial or inflated claims. This demographic values a story that they can believe in and be a part of.

In the context of workplace culture, Gen Z favours collaborative frameworks where ideas around sustainability can be shared and actualised. They thrive in inclusive environments that allow for cross-disciplinary approaches to solve complex environmental and social problems. This amalgamation of skills and perspectives can be a formidable force for innovation within the sustainability sphere.

Moreover, recognition of these efforts matters greatly to Gen Z employees. They're more likely to exhibit loyalty and drive in their roles when they see their work — and its positive impact — being acknowledged. Knowing that their day-to-day tasks contribute to a larger good directly correlates with their job satisfaction and productivity levels.

In sum, the Gen Z mindset places sustainability and social responsibility at the forefront, sculpting new dimensions of corporate engagement in the process. Thriving in this evolving landscape means understanding that for this generation, making a living and making a positive difference in the world are not separate ambitions—they're intrinsically linked. It's not sufficient to have a successful company; for Gen Z, success is measured by how a company enriches the world.

As we look to the future, the challenge and opportunity lie in embracing and nurturing this mindset, recognising its transformative potential. Businesses that can synergise with Gen Z's convictions on sustainability and social responsibility will not only acquire a competitive edge but also contribute to a more resilient, equitable, and eco-conscious world—a legacy that will outlast any single generation's tenure.

Chapter 4: Technological Prowess

With the foundation of intergenerational synergies laid out in the previous chapters, we turn our attention to an unparalleled facet of Generation Z: their technological prowess. Immersed in a digital landscape from the cradle, Gen Z members are synonymous with technology that powers contemporary business. They exhibit a fluency in leveraging tools from AI to VR, intuitively interpreting and manipulating data in ways that signify a paradigm shift within the workforce. They're not merely comfortable with disruptive technologies; they expect them, and more importantly, they can evolve with them, masterfully navigating cybersecurity landscapes while remaining vigilant to privacy concerns. It is imperative for businesses to not only recognise but also embrace and catalyse this competence. Harnessing Gen Z's tech-affinity isn't just about staying current—it's about steering your organisation towards a future where technological adroitness becomes a core competitive asset.

Embracing Disruptive Technologies

In an era where the pace of innovation is relentless, organisations must learn not just to adapt, but to wholeheartedly embrace disruptive technologies. The Gen Z workforce is uniquely positioned to be both the drivers and adopters of groundbreaking tools like AI, blockchain, and IoT, having grown up in a digital maelstrom. Harnessing their inherent proficiency can transform business models, propel productivity, and unlock new avenues for growth. Fostering an environment where ingenuity is aligned with technological fluency will not only satiate the appetite of these young professionals for cutting-edge work but will also give businesses the competitive edge they need in a technologically advanced marketplace. For companies seeking to lead rather than follow, integrating Gen Z's technological prowess into their strategies is not just beneficial—it's imperative.

AI, VR, and the Gen Z Worker

In the arsenal of emerging technologies revolutionising the workplace, Artificial Intelligence (AI) and Virtual Reality (VR) stand out as transformative tools particularly resonant with the Gen Z worker. This demographic, having cut their teeth on digital innovation, enters the workforce not just with a fluency in these technologies but with an expectation of their application in their professional lives.

AI, seen as a driver of efficiency and personalisation, syncs well with Gen Z's desire for streamlined, bespoke work processes and environments. This generation possesses the unique position of being true digital natives, making their integration into an AI-enhanced workplace more intuitive than in previous generations. They're accustomed to machine learning recommendations in every aspect of their lives, from social media feeds to personalised shopping. As such, their transition to AI in the workplace is less a leap and more a step forward.

Similarly, the application of VR in training and development offers an immersive learning experience that ignites the Gen Z passion for innovation. Cutting-edge VR training programs enable young employees to step into realistic simulations, preparing them for real-world scenarios in a risk-free environment. The extensibility of VR goes beyond mere training, it can facilitate remote collaboration, giving teams the semblance of physical presence and the ability to engage with lifelike simulations in real-time.

However, it's not just about integrating the technology, it's about matching it with the Gen Z ethos. This generation prizes work that carries a sense of purpose and value alignment. Therefore, when leveraging AI and VR, businesses must ensure that these tools are used to enhance meaningful work rather than simply replacing human effort with automation.

The juggernaut of connectivity that AI fosters could also positively disrupt how Gen Z employees engage with each other and with external stakeholders. AI-driven platforms enable smarter communication, more agile project management, and a window to global collaboration that reflect the boundless world Gen Z is accustomed to.

Gen Z work dynamics are also deeply influenced by a yearning for a proper work-life balance, well-being, and mental health. AI can play a critical role in providing the analytics required to support these goals. For instance, AI-driven insights can guide HR and leadership to tailor fit wellness programs and identify areas where employees may feel burnt out or disinterested.

As enthusiastic as Gen Z might be towards AI and VR, they are also the most privacy-conscious generation. They understand the power of data and the risks associated with it. Hence, while they may find these technologies inherently appealing, they also demand robust cybersecurity measures to protect their personal and professional data.

Virtual workspaces augmented with VR and AI present a unique opportunity for employee engagement. Gamification, a key motivator for this generation, is exponentially potentiated when combined with VR, turning mundane tasks into interactive experiences that can boost productivity and satisfaction.

Environmental sustainability is another tenant close to the hearts of Gen Z workers, and VR can be a powerful tool in this regard. VR simulations allow for testing and modelling of eco-friendly initiatives in a virtual setting before physical implementation, aligning with Gen Z's mission of environmental responsibility.

But deployment of AI and VR solutions in the workplace isn't merely for direct interaction with Gen Z employees. It is also about preparing businesses for the future. The use of these technologies can streamline operations, enhance customer experiences, and open up new realms of business possibility - arenas where Gen Z will be at the forefront of strategy and execution.

Real-time feedback and analytics are integral components of Gen Z's expectation for growth and skill development. Here, AI becomes an indispensable ally, providing immediate insights into performance, learning progression, and career development paths, facilitating a culture of continuous improvement and feedback.

Considering the impact of these technologies on the Gen Z worker, businesses must be thoughtful in their adoption. It isn't enough to deploy AI and VR for the sake of modernization. These tools should empower, engage, and resonate with a value system that places innovation, ethics, and personal growth at the forefront.

The Gen Z worker thrives in an environment where technology enables them to have their voice heard more loudly, their innovations seen more clearly, and their impact felt more deeply. Companies that harness AI and VR in line with these aspirations will not only attract top-tier Gen Z talent but will also be shaping the future of work in a way that is both revolutionary and deeply humanistic.

These technologies have a role that transcends mere utility. They are vital elements in crafting a workplace that not only meets the business needs of today but is resilient and adaptive to the ever-evolving world of tomorrow - a world in which Gen Z workers are poised to take centre stage.

As we continue to navigate the new paradigms of work, the integration of AI, and VR into our organisational strategies will signify a leap towards a future that Gen Z is already envisioning. Thus, aligning technological advancements with the generational pulse of Gen Z isn't just a business strategy; it's a gateway to perpetuity in an era of unprecedented digital transformation.

Cybersecurity and Privacy Concerns

In the sphere of technological prowess, cybersecurity and privacy concerns form a crucial frontier, especially in the context of integrating Generation Z into the workplace. To put it simply, for a cohort that has grown up in the age of digital revolution, these are not mere bullet points in an employee handbook, they are intrinsic values that shape their interaction with technology. In this section, we delve into the nexus of Gen Z's technological affinity and the imperative of robust cybersecurity and privacy measures, shedding light on the potential risks and opportunities that lie ahead.

Gen Z's digital fluency certainly gives them an edge; however, it also creates a sense of complacency towards potential security threats. With lives enmeshed in the digital sphere, this generation confronts cybersecurity issues as no other generation has before. Through constant connectivity, they are exposed to a plethora of risks – from data breaches and identity theft to more insidious hazards such as cyberbullying and misinformation.

Fostering a safe digital environment is paramount. Organizations must ramp up their cybersecurity infrastructure to safeguard sensitive information, which is frequently the target of malicious attacks. It's not just about firewalls and antivirus software; it's about creating robust protocols that can evolve with threats and educating every layer of the organization, particularly the Gen Z employee, on the importance of vigilant online practices.

Data privacy is another intricate aspect that intertwines with cybersecurity. Gen Z is known for its concerns about privacy, reflecting a pendulum swing from the share-everything approach that characterized some previous generations. The conundrum lies in balancing their desire for personalized experiences with the need for data protection. Addressing this requires transparent policies that spell out how data is collected, used, and protected.

Compliance with data protection regulations, such as the GDPR in the European Union, is non-negotiable. It is essential for organizations to comprehend the legal landscape of privacy and construct compliance frameworks that align with Gen Z's expectations, while simultaneously adhering to international standards. Privacy by design should be at the core of any digital implementation, ensuring that data protection is integrated into the development of business processes.

The proliferation of remote working arrangements presents unique security and privacy challenges. As telecommuting becomes commonplace, it introduces increased risk points, from unsecured networks to the use of personal devices for work purposes. Here, multifactor authentication, secure VPNs, and thorough training become indispensable tools in an organization's security arsenal.

Social engineering attacks such as phishing exploits are becoming more sophisticated, and as Gen Z may perceive themselves as tech-savvy, they could overlook these threats. Vigilance and education must be underscored continuously. Initiatives such as regular security drills and updated training modules help to embed a culture that prioritizes data protection and threat awareness.

Cybersecurity is not solely the domain of IT departments; it's a shared responsibility. Encouraging a culture of security among Gen Z means integrating practices into their workflow seamlessly. Gamification of cybersecurity training can resonate well with this group – by turning learning into an engaging challenge, organizations can enhance the retention and application of security protocols.

In the age of Big Data, organizations collect vast quantities of information, much of it personal. With Gen Z entering the fray, companies must ensure their data collection strategies do not overstep ethical boundaries. Boundaries must be communicated clearly and consent obtained unequivocally. When Gen Zers trust their employers in handling data with integrity, their engagement and loyalty are amplified.

Innovation in cybersecurity measures must match the pace at which technology evolves. Artificial intelligence and machine learning offer proactive ways of identifying potential threats and automating responses. Forward-thinking companies that leverage these technologies position themselves at the vanguard of cybersecurity and, by extension, become more attractive to potential Gen Z talent who value innovative work cultures.

Breaches in cybersecurity not only jeopardize data but can erode trust – a currency of immense value for Gen Z. They seek authenticity and transparency in their professional relationships. A company's response to breaches, therefore, is as significant as its prevention efforts. Crafting comprehensive incident response plans demonstrates a commitment to transparency and fosters resilience in the face of cyber threats.

As Gen Zers champion the cause of digital rights, they are often active proponents against mass surveillance and the misuse of personal data. Businesses need to recognize and appreciate this stance, ensuring that their internal surveillance measures for productivity and security do not infringe upon personal privacy and autonomy.

There is an opportunity for cross-generational learning in cybersecurity. Gen Z's intuitive understanding of technology can be leveraged to educate other generations about digital best practices while older employees can impart wisdom on risk management and professional skepticism. This symbiotic relationship can fortify an organization's overall cyber defense.

Ultimately, the catchphrase 'privacy is priceless' rings true for Gen Z. From a retention perspective, it is crucial that privacy isn't perceived as a forfeitable luxury but as a fundamental right within the workplace. Organizations that earnestly advocate for and uphold cybersecurity and privacy are more likely to engender a strong and committed Gen Z workforce, replete with digital natives poised to steer the company safely through the digital age.

In conclusion, the intersection of Gen Z at the heart of the workforce and the digital transformation of business environments accentuates the significance of cybersecurity and privacy. Striking the proper equilibrium between leveraging technological prowess and securing digital assets against a backdrop of evolving threats will play a pivotal role in ensuring an inclusive and secure future for businesses and their employees alike.

Chapter 5:
Redefining Leadership for Gen Z

Having delved into the technological fluency that defines Generation Z, we pivot to the metamorphosis of leadership that aligns with this cohort's unique expectations. To lead Gen Z effectively, the autocratic paradigms of the past must give way to ecosystems fostering autonomy, transparency, and mutual growth. Gen Z yearns for leaders who aren't just authority figures but collaborators who champion flexibility and imbibe mentorship deeply into their leadership style. For these digital-first trailblazers, leadership isn't just about directing from the helm; it's about being immersed in the trenches, facilitating innovation and advancement through genuine, reciprocal relationships. Leaders will find that by integrating these elements into the workplace culture, not only do they empower Gen Z individuals, but they also fuel an engine of creativity and progress that propels the entire organisation forward.

Cultivating Flexible Hierarchies

As we journey through redefining leadership for an emerging workforce, it's critical to address the structures within which leadership is exercised. For Gen Z, the traditional corporate ladder is a relic of the past. Instead, they seek dynamic and fluid environments where ideas can flow freely and where authority is less about title and more about knowledge and contribution. It's in this context that cultivating flexible hierarchies arises as a strategic imperative for innovative organizations.

Generation Z has grown up in a hyper-connected world where hierarchies are flat and information is democratized. This upbringing has entrenched a preference for egalitarianism and a sceptical view of authority that's tied solely to tenure. They anticipate engaging in spaces that foster collaboration and draw upon diverse strengths, rather than enforcing a strict top-down approach. This inclination offers a fertile ground for nurturing an organizational structure that prizes flexibility over rigidity.

Adopting flexible hierarchies doesn't imply a lack of structure, but rather an adaptive one that's responsive to the needs of the modern project and workforce. It means developing a leadership model in which roles and responsibilities can shift to capitalise on individual strengths. A project lead today may be a supporting team member tomorrow, depending on the demands of the task and the skill set required. This lateral movement emboldens Gen Z to contribute at their highest potential.

Integral to flexible hierarchies is the concept of decentralized decision-making. Companies that empower their employees at all levels to make decisions can enact changes more swiftly and tap into the front-line insights that Gen Z can offer. This autonomy is invigorating for young workers who demand a sense of ownership and direct impact on their work. It also spurs innovation, as ideas aren't bottlenecked awaiting executive approval.

Yet the shift to flexible structures comes with its challenges. For one, the blurring of defined roles can lead to confusion if not managed properly. This can be mitigated by clear communication of temporary roles and responsibilities, aligned with ongoing projects. Training programs must also evolve to equip leaders with the skills to manage fluid teams and foster an environment of mutual respect.

A critical aspect driving the success of flexible hierarchies is an effective feedback loop. Gen Z workers don't just want feedback; they want it to be consistent, constructive, and bidirectional. This fosters a culture of continuous improvement and allows the hierarchy to adapt as required. Smart data and real-time analytics can provide insights into team dynamics and project progress, aiding in informed decision-making.

Through the cultivation of flexible hierarchies, we are not merely addressing Gen Z's preferences; we are also future-proofing our organizations. With the rapid pace of change in technology and global markets, businesses that remain shackled to rigid hierarchies will struggle to keep pace. By contrast, those with the agility that comes from a more fluid structure are better positioned to respond swiftly to emerging challenges and opportunities.

The technology at our disposal today can support such flexible structures. Collaborative platforms enable team members to connect and contribute irrespective of their formal position in the hierarchy. Leaders should leverage these technologies to enhance collaboration, streamline communication, and ensure that vital knowledge isn't siloed within the organization.

Transitioning to a culture that supports flexible hierarchies is a process, not a one-time change. It requires an ongoing commitment to evolution. Leaders must be tenacious in challenging the status quo and persistent in fostering an agile and responsive organizational culture. This necessitates not only structural changes but also a shift in mindset throughout the company.

As for Gen Z, they'll not just fit into these flexible structures — they will thrive and lead within them. By promoting a culture of shared leadership, organizations can draw upon the collective intelligence and creativity of their workforce. Gen Z's comfort with this way of working can transform companies, allowing them to navigate the complexities of the 21st century with dexterity.

This transformation also opens the door for mentorship to take on a new dimension. In fluid hierarchies, mentorship isn't limited to senior staff imparting wisdom but is reciprocal. The cross-pollination of ideas across different levels and departments engenders a well-spring of innovation and deepened understanding of diverse perspectives. This is a cornerstone for the networked approach that Gen Z values highly.

Investment in leadership development must also align with the new realities. Training leaders to facilitate rather than dictate can inspire Gen Z workers to be proactive in taking up roles that suit their competencies regardless of their formal position. This approach affirms their potential to contribute meaningfully, boosting morale and commitment.

Therefore, the symbiosis between Gen Z's expectations and the need for business agility underscores a pivotal point: cultivating flexible hierarchies is not accommodating a new generation's whims — it's strategically aligning with the epochal shifts in the workplace. It's about positioning an organization for innovation, responsiveness, and sustained success.

As we explore the adoption of flexible hierarchies, it's essential for organizations to assess and reassess their internal processes, culture, and technology adoption. Streamlining these aspects to support this new approach to leadership and organization can ultimately create a resilient and progressive company that attracts and retains the best of Gen Z talent.

Finally, embracing flexible hierarchies presents an opportunity for companies to distinguish themselves as leaders in innovation and to construct a workplace environment that not only appeals to Gen Z but also propels the entire organization toward a future of perpetual growth and adaptation. By fostering inclusive, empowering, and dynamic organizational structures, executives and leaders pave the way for a new era of business – one that harnesses the collective strengths and insights of every team member.

Mentorship and Collaborative Growth

As we navigate the nuances of leadership in a world that is increasingly shaped by Generation Z, it becomes apparent that traditional hierarchical structures are being challenged. This generation brings a fresh perspective—one that thirsts for mentorship and thrives on collaboration. The very essence of growth within organisations is being recalibrated to prioritise these elements.

Mentorship, long considered a keystone in the development of young professionals, takes on an invigorated role with Gen Z. Unlike previous generations, for whom mentorship may have been a formal, somewhat stiff relationship, Gen Z envisages mentorship as a dynamic and reciprocal avenue for growth. They look for mentors who are not just superiors imparting wisdom but are also willing to listen and learn from their mentees, forging a two-way street of mutual respect and knowledge exchange.

For forward-thinking leaders, the challenge is to create a mentorship ecosystem that is both structured and flexible, allowing for personal connections and professional development to coexist. This means designing programmes where experience meets innovation, and insights from different generational perspectives are harmonised.

Collaborative growth, interconnected with the notion of mentorship, is another hallmark of Gen Z's influence on the workplace. Collaboration for this cohort is not constrained by job titles or departments. It's a fluid process that seeks to leverage diverse skill sets and ideas to innovate and solve problems. A collaborative growth model thrives on cross-functional teams and project-based work where individuals can contribute irrespective of their position in the company.

Understanding that meaningful collaboration often drives motivation and engagement for Gen Z workers, leaders must foster an environment that not only encourages team-based projects but also recognises and rewards these efforts. It's imperative to dismantle silos and create a culture where open communication and collective brainstorming are the norms rather than the exceptions.

Technological prowess plays a significant role in facilitating this new wave of mentorship and collaboration. The use of digital tools and platforms makes it easier than ever to connect mentors with mentees and to enable teamwork that is not limited by geography or time zones. Effective use of technology promotes inclusivity, allowing ideas to propagate freely across the organisation.

However, it's not enough to merely have the tools for collaboration; they must be harnessed effectively. Gen Z values streamlined processes and user-friendly interfaces, so selecting technology that aligns with these preferences is crucial. Leaders must be discerning, adopting solutions that are intuitive and promote a seamless exchange of ideas.

Professional development is a cornerstone of mentorship and collaborative growth, and Gen Z's appetite for continuous learning and upskilling sets the pace for organisational learning cultures. Training programs ought to be adaptive, blending formal education with real-world application. Allowing Gen Z workers to take charge of their learning paths can lead to better engagement and retention.

This emphasis on development also means reimagining progression within a company. Career ladders may be replaced by career lattices, with opportunities for lateral movement, skill diversification and role variation being as valued as traditional promotions. Such a framework encourages a culture of lifelong learning and a versatile workforce equipped to tackle the challenges of a rapidly evolving business landscape.

Transparency is foundational to mentorship and is necessary for productive collaboration. Gen Z workers seek clear and honest communication about their performance, their career prospects and the health of the business. Leadership must be transparent about both successes and failures to maintain trust and nurture a resilient organisation.

In line with the emphasis on social responsibility prevalent among Gen Z, the alignment of individual and organisational values is integral. Through mentorship, leaders can instil corporate values while also championing the personal goals of their mentees. Similarly, collaborative projects should reflect not only business objectives but also contribute to a broader social good, enticing Gen Z employees who are driven by a purpose beyond profit.

The benefits of this mentorship and collaborative growth model are manifold. Not only does it empower individuals and foster a strong team ethos, but it also catalyses innovation. Gen Z employees often have a distinct, digital-first approach to problem-solving, which can be integrated into company practices through these collaborative efforts.

Moreover, the symbiotic mentorship relationship nurtures future leaders within the organisation. When Gen Z employees are mentored in an environment that values their input, they develop the confidence and competence needed for leadership roles. This paves the way for a seamless generational transition in the company's leadership pipeline.

However, rolling out a successful mentorship and collaborative growth strategy requires care and consideration. Leaders must assess both the needs of Gen Z workers and the capabilities of potential mentors to create meaningful pairings. Similarly, collaboration should not be enforced but encouraged through a blend of incentives that resonate with the values of Gen Z.

In conclusion, redefining leadership for Gen Z means embracing and integrating mentorship and collaborative growth into the fabric of an organisation. A willingness to listen, adapt and grow alongside this newest cohort of the workforce is not merely advantageous—it's essential for any business aiming to remain relevant and vibrant in the face of tomorrow's challenges.

Chapter 6:
Recruitment Strategies for
Attracting Gen Z Talent

In the race to captivate the freshest wave of talent, the strategies employed in recruiting Generation Z need to be as forward-thinking and multifaceted as the generation itself. Building on the strengths and preferences that define Gen Z, recruiters should harness the power of succinct, genuine communication and leverage platforms where these digital natives spend their time. That's not just about posting job ads on social media, but about creating narratives that resonate with them—stories of innovation, flexibility, and ethical business practices. It's about showcasing growth opportunities within the company and emphasising a commitment to sustainability and social responsibility—elements we'll delve deeper into through chapters focused on CSR and workplace design. This generation isn't looking just for a job; they're searching for a place where they can make a tangible impact, align with their values, and continuously learn and adapt. The nuances of wooing this capable cohort go beyond mere job descriptions; they hinge on a company's ability to project its culture and values through every touchpoint, building not just a workforce but a community that's ready to tackle the challenges of a rapidly evolving business landscape.

Effective Communication Techniques

In navigating the nuanced landscape of Gen Z recruitment, robust communication methods are paramount. With this cohort steering away from traditional corporate jargon, a fresh, sincere tone is necessary—a blend of formality and casualness that resonates. Emphasising visual and interactive storytelling will often strike a chord, as this generation grew up on platforms where visual media reigns supreme. Timely feedback and ongoing dialogue, fostered through channels they frequent, underpin the engagement process. It's about crafting a narrative that's not only compelling but also reflective of their personal values and the role they aspire to play within your organisation. Transparency is king; vague promises won't hold water with a demographic that values stark honesty. Practicing active listening across various digital mediums solidifies trust and demonstrates respect for their opinions and ideas. In essence, optimising communication with Gen Z means ensuring every exchange is meaningful, multi-channelled, and meticulously tailored to echo their voices, not just echo corporate objectives.

Leveraging Social Media and Digital Platforms

In the realm of modern recruitment, social media and digital platforms stand as the crucial battlegrounds for attracting top-tier Generation Z talent. As cognisant digital natives, this cohort has a natural affinity for online spaces, making them an indispensable resource for organisations looking to cultivate a forward-thinking workforce. Digital platforms are not merely channels for socialising for Gen Z but are the very fabric of their daily lives – for learning, shopping, entertainment, and significantly, for career prospects.

It's essential to recognise that social media for Gen Z goes beyond the traditional suspects such as Facebook or Twitter. They have grown up immersed in the visual storytelling of Instagram, the spontaneous creativity of TikTok, and the professional networking sphere of LinkedIn. Each of these platforms offers unique advantages. Instagram can showcase company culture through vivid imagery and stories, TikTok can humanise your brand through relatable content, and

LinkedIn remains the stronghold for professional branding and networking.

To truly harness the potential of these platforms, companies must develop a strategic approach. This means moving away from one-size-fits-all job postings and towards bespoke content that resonates with this generation's values and lifestyle. Authenticity here is key; contrived content will likely be dismissed by savvy Gen Zers who can sniff out inauthenticity from a mile away.

Content strategies on digital platforms must also be adaptive, integrating real-time feedback and engagement metrics. Gen Z appreciates brands that listen and evolve. When they comment on a post or share their views, they want to see that they're not only heard but also considered. This two-way dialogue builds trust and a sense of community, which is especially important in a corporate context to attract potential Gen Z employees who value meaningful interactions.

Companies should also be utilising employee advocacy programs, where current Gen Z staff share their experiences and insights. This peer-to-peer influence is incredibly powerful as potential recruits see the reality of working with you through the lens of their contemporaries. Broadcasting the voices of your Gen Z employees not only provides transparency but also strengthens your brand's relevance.

User-generated content campaigns can greatly amplify recruitment efforts. By encouraging current employees to share their work-life moments, companies can display authenticity and create relatable content that appeals to Gen Z's desire for a realistic preview of their potential work environment. These organic insights can serve as testimonials to your organisation's commitment to a vibrant and supportive workplace.

Moreover, it's vital to remember that a mobile-first approach is non-negotiable. Gen Z spends a significant amount of time on their smartphones. Hence, ensuring that all digital content, especially job postings and application processes, is mobile-friendly is of the utmost importance. An application process that is cumbersome on mobile devices is likely to deter potential candidates right from the start.

Data analytics also plays a pivotal role in fine-tuning recruitment strategies on social media and digital platforms. By tracking engagement rates, click-through rates, and conversion rates, HR teams can identify what types of content work best and when to post them for maximum impact. The use of analytics can inform not just a powerful strategy for attracting Gen Z workers but also for continuous improvement and adaption to the evolving digital landscape.

Creative campaigns that utilise social media challenges, hashtags, and interactive elements can further boost visibility and engagement. Given Gen Z's affinity for collaboration and interaction, these tactics can turn passive browsing into active participation. Whether it's through hosting a virtual career fair on Reddit or a hashtag challenge on TikTok, engagement that entertains as it informs can significantly lift your employer brand in the eyes of Gen Z.

With all these efforts, it's crucial to create a consistent omnichannel presence. Gen Z interacts with brands across various platforms and expects a uniform experience whether they're scrolling through Instagram, tweeting, or updating their LinkedIn profile. A disjointed brand presence can cause confusion and dilute trust – cardinal sins in the eyes of a generation that prioritises authenticity and transparency.

Cybersecurity is another aspect of digital platforms that cannot be overlooked. With Gen Z's acute awareness of data privacy and online safety, organisations must demonstrate their commitment to protecting personal information. A solid reputation for cybersecurity can be a determining factor for Gen Z candidates considering your company as their employer.

Finally, a focus on social listening tools will allow companies to stay abreast of the changing preferences and dialogues within Gen Z communities. Social listening goes beyond monitoring brand mentions and delves deeper into understanding the sentiments and discussions that prevail among potential Gen Z recruits. This intel is invaluable for tweaking your digital recruitment strategy to align with the ever-changing digital zeitgeist.

Integration of these elements – authenticity in content, analytics to guide strategy, creative campaigns for high engagement, a consistent omnichannel presence, commitment to cybersecurity, and a finger on the pulse of trends through social listening – will culminate in a robust digital recruitment approach. This is critical for organisations aiming to attract and integrate Gen Z into their workforce.

Organisations that are successful in leveraging social media and digital platforms demonstrate a deep understanding of Gen Z's world. They treat these platforms not just as tools for outreach, but as integral parts of their organisational culture and brand identity. By doing so, they not only attract Generation Z talents but also position themselves as leaders in an increasingly digital-centric business landscape.

Chapter 7:
Designing Gen Z-Friendly Workspaces

In a landscape where generational distinctions profoundly affect workplace design, creating spaces that resonate with the aspirations of Generation Z has become imperative. Integrating their preference for collaborative and agile environments, executives and HR strategists must envision workplaces that not only foster collaboration but also offer the dichotomy of personalisation and community. This chapter takes a closer look at how offices can be tailored to the wants and needs of this emerging workforce. Gen Z's predilection for versatility in working patterns demands spaces that bridge the gap between physical presence and the digital world they fluently inhabit. Therefore, the ideal environment seamlessly blends areas for concentration and creativity with versatile technology-ready nooks, facilitating both independent innovation and dynamic teamwork. Balancing physical and remote work arrangements isn't just a concession to contemporary trends; it's a strategic move to engage the digitally-savvy Gen Z in their natural habitat. The nuanced intrigue in this chapter revolves around how these functional spaces can be refined to bolster wellbeing alongside productivity, and how spacial design reflects an organisation's broader values of inclusivity and sustainability. By the chapter's end, leaders will be equipped with a clear blueprint for moulding workspaces that not only attract but retain the brightest of Generation Z, setting a new standard in workplace evolution.

Creating Collaborative and Agile Environments

As we delve deeper into the requisites of designing Gen Z-friendly workspaces, it becomes increasingly apparent that fostering collaborative and agile environments is not just a preference but a necessity. The young workforce entering the professional realm brings with it a fresh set of expectations and working styles. They thrive in settings that are less hierarchical and more supportive of quick pivoting and cross-functional teamwork.

Collaboration is not merely about working side by side; it is about creating a synergistic atmosphere where each individual can contribute openly and sincerely. Gen Z values transparency, and as such, workspaces that facilitate this through open-plan designs and communal areas are favourable. These aren't just spaces; they are breeding grounds for innovation where spontaneous meetings can spark the next great idea.

Agility, another cornerstone of the modern workspace, is more than a buzzword for today's young professionals. It's a way of operating that accommodates rapid change and diverse project demands. Gen Z employees have grown up in a world where change is the only constant, and their workplaces need to reflect this reality. Agile workspaces are designed with flexibility in mind, equipped to adapt to various tasks and team sizes at a moment's notice.

One can't discuss agility without mentioning technology. As digital natives, Gen Zers expect the latest tech solutions to be embedded into their work environments. These tools not only empower them to work efficiently but also contribute to a culture of innovation and continual learning that they find particularly attractive.

But technology alone doesn't make a collaborative environment. The social aspect of the workspace is just as critical. Designing for interaction, whether through informal lounge areas or communal worktables, encourages Gen Zers to mingle and exchange ideas outside the constraints of formal meetings or emails.

Environmental adaptability plays a central role in maintaining an agile workspace. Modular furniture, sit-stand desks, and multipurpose areas ensure that the space can be reconfigured for different types of work, from individual focussed tasks to collaborative workshops. Such fluidity is essential, catering to both the task at hand and the diverse working preferences of Gen Z.

The concept of 'work anywhere' has been embraced eagerly by this generation. This translates to the need for versatile areas within the office that mimic the comfort of a living room or the buzz of a café, fostering a sense of freedom and independence that Gen Z values highly.

It's not just about physical space when curating an agile and collaborative environment; it's also about fostering the right mindset. Gen Z workers are looking for a culture that encourages them to take initiative, experiment, and even fail safely. Empowering them with a degree of autonomy not only motivates but also harnesses their entrepreneurial spirit.

Leadership styles within collaborative and agile workspaces are also evolving. Rather than authoritative figures, leaders are expected to be facilitators and coaches, aiding Gen Z employees in their career paths and helping them navigate through organisational complexities.

Creating a sense of community is essential for nurturing a collaborative culture. This involves not just professional development opportunities but also social and wellness activities that bring employees together, helping build stronger, more cohesive teams.

Feedback mechanisms are vital in any agile environment. Gen Z workers expect continuous dialogue rather than annual reviews.

Implementing real-time feedback tools enables quick adjustments and keeps teams aligned with shifting goals and priorities.

Similarly, understanding the unique communication styles of Gen Z is paramount. They are native users of instant messaging and social media, and these channels are often their default for interaction. Integration of these tools into the workplace can significantly elevate collaboration and responsiveness.

In line with this communication style, workspaces must support a blend of virtual and physical interactions. Flexibility in terms of telecommuting options is necessary, but so are high-quality video conferencing facilities that allow seamless communication with remote team members and external partners.

Lastly, it's crucial to consider the environmental impact of our agile and collaborative spaces. Sustainability matters greatly to Gen Z, and workspace designs should incorporate eco-friendly materials, energy-efficient systems, and recycling programs that resonate with their values.

In conclusion, creating a workspace that appeals to Gen Z is about crafting an ecosystem that is as dynamic and multifaceted as they are. It's about designing for transparency, agility, and technology integration while nurturing a culture that highly values interaction, feedback, and community. These are the workspaces that will not only attract but also retain the best young talent in the years to come.

Balancing Physical and Remote Work Arrangements

In designing workspaces that resonate with Gen Z, it is critical to strike the right balance between physical and remote work arrangements. This generation has grown up in a hyper-connected world, where digital communication is often as natural as face-to-face interaction. They envision work environments that are not only technologically adept but also flexible in terms of where and how work can be conducted.

Gen Z's preferences are driving a significant shift away from the traditional 9-to-5 office model towards more dynamic, hybrid arrangements. These arrangements acknowledge the variety of workstyles and environments in which this generation thrives. They are adept at using technology to complete tasks from virtually anywhere, provided they have access to the internet. Hence, workspaces must evolve to include versatile areas that cater to both collaborative and independent work.

A forward-thinking executive must consider how their organisation's workspace can offer flexibility while still fostering a sense of community and collaboration among employees. Flexible workstations, communal areas, quiet zones, and technology-equipped meeting rooms are all essential components of this hybrid model. The physical office space should be adaptable, allowing for personalisation according to the task or project at hand.

However, the shift towards remote work arrangements does not solely focus on the physical design of workspaces. It also encompasses the policies and culture that underpin an organisation's approach to work. Enabling remote work requires a robust IT infrastructure that ensures security, reliability, and ease of access for all employees.

Moreover, building a culture that genuinely supports remote work is paramount. It's not just about having the right tools; it's also about nurturing trust and accountability. Gen Z workers seek autonomy but they also crave meaningful engagement with their peers and superiors. Thus, maintaining a sense of connection and community, even in a distributed workforce, is vital.

Companies can harness virtual communication tools, like video conferencing and real-time collaboration platforms, to bridge the gap between remote and in-office teams. However, those tools alone don't assure effective collaboration. Clear communication protocols, regular check-ins, and virtual team-building activities contribute significantly to a cohesive remote work culture.

On the flip side, a purely remote setup isn't the panacea for all workspace challenges. Physical offices offer tangible benefits in terms of spontaneity, informal networking, and serendipitous innovation that can sometimes be lost in digital translation. Therefore, it is not about favouring one over the other but integrating both to harness their unique advantages.

One way to facilitate this integration is by creating 'satellite' workspaces that provide localised opportunities for remote employees to gather and collaborate when necessary. This not only reduces the sense of isolation often associated with remote work but also leverages the potential for creative synergy in physical gatherings.

An organisation's leadership must establish clarity around when and why employees are expected to be in the office. Is it for team meetings, client presentations, or collaborative projects? Having clear guidelines helps manage expectations and allows Gen Z employees to plan their work schedules effectively.

Monitoring performance in a hybrid workspace can be challenging, but it need not rely solely on in-person oversight. Performance metrics should be results-oriented, focusing on outcomes rather than hours logged. This approach suits the Gen Z workforce's desire for autonomy and is in line with modern productivity philosophies.

Companies should not overlook the environmental implications of their remote work policies. Gen Z is particularly conscious of sustainability, so promoting remote work can align with reducing an organisation's carbon footprint. Fewer commutes mean less pollution and a smaller carbon footprint, which can bolster a company's environmental credentials.

Finally, an executive must remember that these strategies should not be static. Regular feedback from employees, including surveys and discussions, will help fine-tune the balance between remote and physical workspace elements. It is through continuous engagement with Gen Z workers that organizations can remain agile and responsive to the evolving needs of their workforce.

In sum, crafting a workspace for Gen Z is as much about culture as it is about architecture. It's about creating an ecosystem that supports fluid movement between different working styles and environments. It's about recognising that productivity isn't confined to a traditional office setup and that innovation can thrive in a variety of settings.

Embracing the complexity of balancing physical and remote work arrangements is not a simple task, yet it is the crucible in which future-proof workplaces are forged. The payoff for getting it right is a resilient, inclusive, and dynamic workspace that not only attracts Gen Z talent but also propels an organisation towards a vibrant future.

Chapter 8:
Training and Development for a New Era

In the unfolding narrative of integrating Generation Z into the workforce, Chapter 8 serves as a pivotal moment where traditional methods of training and development undergo a transformative realignment. As we explore the contours of this new era, it's incumbent upon us to craft learning opportunities that are not simply incremental, but revolutionary, in their design. Gen Z's arrival into the workplace isn't just a gentle ripple—it's a profound tide reshaping every fundamental aspect of on-the-job growth. Therefore, it is indispensable that learning programs are as agile and tech-savvy as the young minds they aspire to develop. This chapter delves into reinventing these programs, presenting a paradigm where microlearning isn't just an option, but a necessity, serving up bite-sized, yet comprehensive educational experiences that resonate with a generation whose lives are a tapestry of interconnected digital threads.

Tailoring Learning Opportunities

In the increasingly diverse landscape of contemporary training and development, it's imperative we craft learning opportunities that resonate with the mores and learning styles of Generation Z. As we segue into a new epoch, our educational methodologies must evolve, substantiating an environment that duly reflects the agility and tech-savviness of our youngest workforce members. This necessitates the judicious deployment of an eclectic mixture of interactive platforms and cutting-edge learning techniques that not only kindle the innate curiosity of Gen Z but also foster a flexible and continuous learning ethos, which flawlessly syncs with their digital upbringing. Our strategic intention is clear: to design and implement learning modules that are incrementally challenging, profoundly relevant, and unequivocally captivating, thereby assuring that these rising stars remain perennially engaged, exceptionally well-prepared, and unfailingly at the spearhead of innovation and organisational evolution.

Microlearning and Its Benefits

As we delve into the training and development strategies that resonate with Generation Z, it's critical to spotlight microlearning—a contemporary approach that dovetails elegantly with the inclinations and learning habits of this digitally adept generation. The concept of microlearning hinges on the delivery of content in small, focused chunks, making it highly digestible and congruent with the on-demand, byte-sized consumption patterns prominent among Gen Zers.

Microlearning emerges as an efficient tool to specifically tailor training experiences that align with the shorter attention spans but quicker processing abilities observed in Gen Z learners. These condensed learning modules can be consumed rapidly, often in minutes, allowing for learning to slot neatly into the everyday flow of life without demanding protracted periods of concentration.

The benefits of microlearning extend beyond its match with generational preferences—it's a paradigm that honours the principle of spaced repetition. This pedagogical approach suggests that information is more effectively retained when revisited over spaced intervals. By leveraging this with microlearning, organisations fortify the long-term retention of skills and knowledge, which is essential in the fast-evolving business landscape where Gen Z is poised to excel.

Access to microlearning can be via diverse platforms, whether through mobile applications, intranet resources or even social media, offering Gen Z instant access to the learning resources that they desire. This ubiquitous availability caters to their preference for seamless and integrated learning experiences that blend with their agile work styles.

Moreover, microlearning is particularly adaptable and can be frequently updated or expanded to include the latest industry developments or technological advancements. This keeps the Gen Z workforce at the vanguard of emerging trends, which not only enhances their job performance but also fuels their innate desire for growth and learning.

Considering Gen Z's environmental and social consciousness, microlearning also stands out as an eco-friendlier alternative to traditional training methods. Reducing the need for printed materials and the associated logistics of in-person training sessions reflects a commitment to sustainability that resonates with this cohort's values.

Customisation and personalisation are central to microlearning's appeal, as modules can be designed to adapt to the individual learner's progress and proficiency. This personalised learning journey is conducive to improved engagement and mastery of skills, as it empowers Gen Z learners to take the reins of their development trajectory.

From an organisational viewpoint, microlearning represents a cost-effective solution for employee training. Reducing the need for extensive face-to-face training sessions diminishes associated costs while still achieving the desired uplift in skills and competencies. This, coupled with the potential for increased productivity through targeted learning interventions, makes microlearning an attractive proposition.

Microlearning inherently facilitates a more focused approach to professional development. By tackling one competency at a time, Gen Z employees are empowered to apply what they've learned immediately, translating new knowledge into practical, on-the-job enhancements. This immediate application not only reinforces learning but also provides tangible benefits to the business through the continual upskilling of the workforce.

From the standpoint of organizational strategy, microlearning enables continuous learning, a cornerstone in building a resilient and adaptable workforce. This approach nurtures a culture where learning is embedded within the workflow, promoting a mindset aligning with Gen Z's expectations of perpetual growth and progression.

Analytics play a pivotal role in the success of microlearning initiatives. With data-driven insights, organisations can evaluate the effectiveness of each module, ensuring content remains relevant and impactful. This analytical framework aligns with Gen Z's comfort around data and technology, offering a transparent view into their own learning progress and outcomes—a key motivator for this generation.

The collaborative potential inherent in microlearning channels should not be underestimated. Social features like forums or chat functionalities attached to learning modules, provide Gen Z a platform to discuss, share, and enrich their learning experience collectively. This aligns with their preference for collaborative and networked working styles, fostering a sense of community within the learning environment.

Embedding microlearning within career development pathways offers Gen Z employees a clear visual of how their learning contributes to their career progression within the organisation. This tangibility of learning outcomes fuels their ambition and demonstrates an organisational commitment to their development and future roles, thus enhancing retention and morale.

Lastly, microlearning aligns with the just-in-time performance support preferred by Gen Z employees. When faced with a challenge, they can quickly access relevant learning nuggets that offer immediate guidance or solutions, thereby reducing downtime and enhancing productivity.

In conclusion, microlearning is not just an adjunct to traditional training methods; it is transformative. For forward-thinking businesses seeking to integrate and elevate their Gen Z workforce, microlearning stands as a robust pillar in the architecture of modern learning and development. It reflects an astute recognition of generational learning preferences, technological fluidity, and the need for continuous innovation — and positions organisations to bask in the multitude of benefits that ensue.

Chapter 9:
Communication in a
Multi-Generational Workplace

Recognising the nuances of communication that resonate distinctly across different generations is fundamental in cultivating a thriving, age-diverse workplace. Gen Z's entry into the professional arena has ushered in novel communication paradigms, necessitating a shift away from conventional practices to ensure that every voice is heard and valued. The crux of Chapter 9 lies in distilling effective strategies that address and harmonise the disparate communication styles that come with a multi-generational talent pool. Through exploring intelligent tools and inventive platforms, this chapter delves into how seamless collaboration can be achieved, irrespective of age-related communication preferences. The aim is to equip organisations with the knowledge to facilitate an exchange of ideas that transcends generational gaps, enhancing innovation while fostering a culture of mutual respect and understanding. As Gen Z carves out their niche in professional settings, their penchant for immediacy and transparency in communication is challenging establishments to rethink and reinvent dialogue within their teams, underlining the imperative for adaptive, cross-generational fluency in the modern workplace.

Harmonising Diverse Communication Styles

In the zeitgeist of a multi-generational workplace, harmonising communication styles has never been more paramount. Each generation brings its own set of preferences, shaped by socio-cultural trends and technological advancements. To foster a truly inclusive environment, businesses must understand and integrate these divergent communication modalities into a coherent whole, especially when considering the entrance of Generation Z into the professional arena.

Generation Z, the cohort born from the mid-1990s onwards, has emerged as the most internet-savvy and digitally fluent generation in history. Their upbringing in a hyper-connected world implies that their preferred methods of communication are fast, visual, and mobile-centric. Consequently, traditional email chains and formal reports may not resonate with them as effectively as they do with Baby Boomers or Gen Xers, who value detailed, linear communication.

It's not merely about preferences; diverse communication styles can significantly impact workplace dynamics. Gen Zers might favour instant messaging and social media platforms for swift and informal interactions, while Millennials might lean towards collaborative tools that allow for seamless sharing and co-working. Such differences, if left unmanaged, can lead to miscommunication and a sense of disconnect among team members.

To harmonise these styles, it behoves leadership to understand the strengths each generation brings to the table. Baby Boomers often provide comprehensive insights and value face-to-face communication, while Millennials and Gen Xers might excel in bridging digital and in-person interactions. Generation Z's proficiency with digital media can inject speed and innovation into workplace communications.

One approach to fostering harmonious communication is to establish a tiered communication protocol. This means identifying and agreeing on which platforms are used for different types of communication. For instance, important announcements might be made over email, which provides a formal record, while day-to-day collaboration could take place in project management apps or chat platforms that Gen Zers might find more engaging.

In cultivating this environment, regular workshops and training sessions can play a key role. Older generations might require upskilling in the latest communication tools, while younger workers may benefit from understanding the importance of formality and clarity in certain business contexts. Such training helps to create a common ground where everyone feels confident in both sending and receiving messages through the preferred channels of their colleagues.

Open forums for discussion enable employees from all generations to voice their preferences and concerns, contributing to a live dialogue about effective communication. By encouraging an exchange of methodologies, employees can co-create a hybrid communication culture that leverages the best practices from each generational group.

It's crucial to acknowledge that while digital means of communication are efficient, they are not a substitute for the human touch that comes with face-to-face interactions. Thus, creating opportunities for in-person or video conferencing can aid in building rapport and understanding across different age groups within the workplace.

A mentoring program can also be beneficial, pairing younger Gen Z employees with experienced professionals. This not only facilitates the sharing of communication norms across generations but also helps build mutual respect and understanding. It allows older employees to stay current with evolving communication trends, while younger employees gain insights into the nuanced approaches that have stood the test of time.

Leadership must lead by example, and in the context of communication, this means adopting a versatile communication style. Leaders who are adept at switching between modes and platforms inspire their teams to do the same. Moreover, they can act as mediators in translating the implicit norms and values embedded in each generation's communicative approach.

Data-driven strategies can also be employed to fine-tune the harmonisation of communication styles. By collecting feedback and analysing communication patterns within the organisation, leaders can make informed decisions about which practices to adopt, adjust, or discard.

It's not enough to simply introduce diverse communication tools; a sustainable approach requires embedding flexibility into the company culture. Policies and protocols should allow employees to adapt their communication style to the context and the needs of their teams, promoting a dynamic and responsive communication landscape.

Finally, celebrating successful communication as part of a company's accomplishments fosters a sense of pride in the collective ability to converse and connect across generational lines. Sharing stories of successful multi-generational projects can serve as inspirational case studies for the rest of the company.

In conclusion, harmonising diverse communication styles is an ongoing process that demands attention, intention, and dedication. By embracing the wealth of perspectives across generations, businesses can create a cohesive, vibrant communications ecosystem that not only resonates with Generation Z but enhances the collaborative spirit of the entire workforce. It's an investment in the company's social capital that will undoubtedly yield dividends in innovation, productivity, and employee satisfaction.

Tools and Platforms for Seamless Collaboration

In the tapestry of the multi-generational workplace, the tools and platforms for seamless collaboration are akin to the threads that bind different swatches of fabric into a single, cohesive material. As we navigate the complex mesh of communications in a workplace teeming with diversity, it's imperative to dwell on the role technology plays in bridging the generational divide.

For Gen Z, who are entering the workforce with an appetite for fluid, agile interactions, digital platforms are a native tongue. Therefore, championing tools that resonate with this digital dexterity while also catering to the preferences of older generations can propel an organisation towards harmonious productivity. Respecting this, let us explore the arsenal of collaboration platforms that cater to a varied workforce.

Instant messaging tools have gained immense traction as a medium offering the immediacy and informality that Generation Z thrives on. Slack, Microsoft Teams, and similar platforms enable real-time communication, responses at one's own pace, and the curation of topic-specific channels which can cut across the hierarchical layers of an organisation.

However, when it comes to more structured communication, project management tools like Asana, Trello, and Monday.com pave the way for clear task delineation and progress tracking. They can reduce email clutter—a boon for Gen Z who often perceive emails as a less dynamic mode of communication—and provide a visual roadmap aligning teams of all ages towards common goals.

Video conferencing tools such as Zoom, Google Meet, or Microsoft Teams again cater to a human need for visual interaction, which became paramount during the shift to remote work. For Gen Z, this not only replicates the face-to-face experience they value but also introduces a platform for expressive, dynamic sharing of ideas without geographical constraints.

On the flip side, collaborative document editing and file sharing platforms, such as Google Workspace or Microsoft 365, offer the advantage of concurrent editing and version control, eliminating the silos that can impede cross-generational collaboration. They encourage pairing of minds: the experienced with fresh perspectives and the energetic with the strategic.

It's worth noting that collaboration goes beyond just project management and communication. Learning Management Systems (LMS), like Coursera for Business or LinkedIn Learning, are integral in nurturing a culture of continuous development, highly valued by Gen Z. These can be avenues for upskilling, shared across generations, fostering a collective growth mindset.

Furthermore, adoption of Customer Relationship Management (CRM) platforms, such as Salesforce or HubSpot, demonstrates a commitment to harnessing information and interaction data to one's advantage, an analytical pursuit that Gen Z finds invigorating, and older generations recognise as business critical.

Technology also has a role in fostering informal interactions through platforms like Donut, which pairs employees randomly for coffee chats, addressing a Gen Z penchant for networking and serendipitous learning, while older colleagues appreciate the chance to broaden their professional relationships within the company.

The social intranet platforms, such as Jive or Yammer, can also serve as digital watercoolers. They're a nod to traditional office culture, providing all staff, irrespective of age or tenure, a space to disseminate information, celebrate wins, and solidify a sense of community.

Integration tools act as the arbiters in a world dense with different software. Zapier, for instance, can streamline workflows by automating tasks across apps, which serves to heighten efficiency—a common goal that cuts through generational preferences and needs.

Sophisticated design and prototyping tools like Adobe XD, Figma, and Sketch invite collaboration at a visual and intuitive level. Gen Z's affinity for aesthetics and UX design means that tools which allow co-creation and instant feedback resonate deeply with their working style, and multigenerational teams can benefit from this visually rich dialogue.

Lastly, embracing platforms dedicated to recognition and rewards, such as Bonusly, addresses the human need for appreciation, an aspect imperative for motivation and engagement across all generations. When individuals of all ages feel seen and valued, the stage is set for collaboration to truly thrive.

One must not forget that the selection and implementation of these tools should be strategised with inclusivity in mind. Training should be provided where necessary, ensuring all employees are equipped to use the chosen platforms to their full potential, thereby negating any sense of alienation.

The modern workspace is indeed a mosaic of generations, each with varying experiences and expectations. It is through the lens of these collaborative tools and platforms, carefully selected and effectively utilised, that we can hope to achieve the unity necessary to forge ahead. It's a concerted effort to embrace the legacy and innovative potential within every team, facilitating a workplace that leads with its diversity as its strength.

Chapter 10:
Engaging Gen Z Employees

As we navigate the subtleties of intergenerational dynamics within the workplace, it becomes particularly crucial to tailor engagement strategies to the unique attributes of Gen Z employees. A confluence of technological adeptness and a yearning for authentic collaboration defines this cohort—attributes that, when leveraged astutely, can significantly bolster a company's innovative capacity and workplace vitality. At the heart of engaging these young talents lies the importance of establishing a feedback-rich environment where recognition is not only expected but intricately woven into the fabric of daily operations. To resonate with the Gen Z ethos, forward-thinking organisations are moving beyond conventional reward systems, instead exploring the potential of gamification to spark motivation and drive performance. This chapter delves into these methodologies, shedding light on how feedback loops and incentivisation mechanics can be transformed into powerful engagement catalysts that align with the passion and vibrancy of the Gen Z workforce.

Building a Culture of Feedback and Recognition

In nurturing an environment that is welcoming to Generation Z employees, it's imperative to acknowledge their inclination towards instant feedback and recognition. This cohort has grown up with instant responses at their fingertips and expects a similar immediacy in the workplace. To engage these young professionals effectively, a culture that supports continuous feedback and celebrates achievements must be cultivated.

Recognition in the workplace isn't merely an optional perk for Gen Z; it's a fundamental aspect of their job satisfaction. This generation wants to know that their work doesn't just exist in a vacuum—they seek tangible, visible signs of their impact. Establishing a feedback-rich environment, therefore, isn't indulgence but a strategic move to maintain employee engagement and retention.

For Gen Z, authentic recognition outranks empty praise. Authenticity means that appreciation must be specific, meaningful, and appropriate. Blanket statements and generic reward systems do little to motivate them. Instead, tailor feedback to the individual, aligning it with their personal goals and the specifics of their contributions. This nuanced approach not only reinforces their work's value but also demonstrates an investment in their professional growth.

Gen Z employees thrive on continuous learning, and feedback plays a crucial role in this process. A forward-thinking organisation must establish a mechanism where feedback isn't just an annual occurrence but a daily practice. This can range from simple check-ins to refined peer review systems. The key is embedding feedback loops into the natural working rhythm, ensuring it's constructive and targeted towards development.

Technology obviously intersects with the way Gen Z expects to receive feedback. Digital platforms that facilitate real-time communication can be leveraged for delivering instant responses. From project management tools with commenting features to dedicated platforms for employee recognition, the digital fluency of Gen Z should be mirrored in the way feedback is structured.

Cross-generational collaboration within the workplace presents an invaluable opportunity for mutual learning. Gen Z can benefit from the experience and insight of older generations, while their unique perspective can stimulate fresh approaches to problem-solving. Establishing mentorship programs that encourage a reciprocal exchange of feedback can be particularly effective.

However, for recognition to be truly impactful, it must go beyond verbal affirmation. Innovating new forms of rewards that resonate with Gen Z's values—such as opportunities for upskilling, flexible work arrangements, or contributions to causes they care about—can amplify the effectiveness of such acknowledgment.

Moreover, fostering an atmosphere where feedback is not just top-down but multidirectional empowers Gen Z employees to actively participate in shaping their work environment. This could be facilitated through regular town hall meetings, suggestion boxes, or digital channels encouraging open dialogue.

Peer recognition is also an essential component of a holistic feedback environment. Gen Z workers value the opinions of their co-workers significantly, often equating peer validation with their sense of professional worth. Encouraging a peer-to-peer recognition scheme can strengthen team bonds and build a supportive community within the workplace.

It's also crucial to remember that feedback should be balanced. While positive reinforcement is vital, constructive criticism, when delivered thoughtfully, can foster resilience and the capacity for self-improvement in the Gen Z workforce.

Celebrating milestone achievements, either through formal awards or informal gatherings, can have a profound impact on Gen Z's overall work experience. Achieving a balance between regular recognition and exceptional celebrations will ensure the continued motivation of these employees.

However, in the pursuit of building a feedback culture, it's important to avoid falling into the trap of micromanagement. Feedback should empower rather than constrain. Helping workers understand the 'why' behind the feedback gives them the autonomy to adjust their actions and aligns them more closely with organisational goals.

For all these strategies to be effective, feedback and recognition must be genuinely embedded into the corporate culture, rather than being an afterthought. Leadership buy-in is crucial to this end. When leaders exemplify the feedback culture by actively participating and valuing it, it sets the tone for the entire organization.

In conclusion, to engage a generation that has been weaned on the instantaneity of digital communication while upholding meaningful work relations, the feedback and recognition systems within a company must be prompt, sincere, and tailored. A well-thought-out system of continuous, multi-directional feedback will not only meet the expectations of Gen Z but will also foster a dynamic, innovative, and collaborative workplace for all generations.

Gamification and Employee Motivation

Efficiently engaging Gen Z employees requires innovative approaches that resonate with their digital fluency and hunger for instant feedback. Gamification, the process of integrating game mechanics into non-game contexts, such as tasks and challenges in the workplace, emerges as a compelling strategy to enhance motivation and participation among this cohort. By tapping into the innate human desire for competition, reward, and recognition, gamification transforms mundane tasks into compelling activities.

Gen Z, growing up amidst an abundance of interactive technology and social media, responds positively to environments that mimic these experiences. They're accustomed to the instant gratification that comes from video games and online interactions, where actions are immediately rewarded and progress is visibly tracked. Adapting these elements into the workplace can increase the appeal of tasks and milestones, motivating Gen Z employees to engage more deeply with their work.

However, successful gamification isn't as simple as one might assume. It's not just about adding points or leaderboards to tasks; it's about embracing a nuanced understanding of what drives Gen Z and how they interact with gaming elements. The key lies in creating meaningful challenges that align with the organization's goals and the individual's personal and career aspirations.

One effective facet of gamification is goal-setting. Constructing clear, attainable goals within a game-like framework empowers employees to take ownership of their objectives. For Gen Z, this means showcasing a pathway for growth and offering transparency in how their efforts contribute to larger company ambitions. A tiered system of achievements, badges, or levels can enable employees to track their progress in real-time, fostering a sense of accomplishment.

Feedback loops are another crucial component. Immediate and ongoing feedback, similar to the instant updates received in games, keeps Gen Z employees informed about their performance. This continual loop not only enhances learning and adaptation but also provides the kind of engagement that Gen Z values. Rewards for achieving certain milestones or improving skills serve both to recognize individual effort and to encourage continued commitment.

Collaborative competition, or team-based challenges, aligns with Gen Z's preference for group interaction and social connectivity. This approach fosters a sense of community and collective achievement. By designing gamified projects that require collaboration, companies can leverage Gen Z's competitive spirit in a way that bolsters team dynamics and contributes to a productive workplace culture.

Customizability is essential when introducing gamification into the workplace. What motivates one employee may not necessarily resonate with another. Providing options for Gen Z workers to personalize their gamified experience ensures higher engagement and better outcomes. Whether it's choosing which rewards to aim for or selecting the type of challenges they want to tackle, autonomy plays a significant role in employee motivation.

It's also crucial to ensure that gamification aligns with the intrinsic values of Gen Z. This generation is purpose-driven, and if they perceive activities as lacking substance or as disconnected from real-world impact, they're likely to disengage. Meaningful gamification marries the competitiveness and fun of games with genuine progress and development within their roles and the wider organisation.

Technology plays a critical role in deploying gamification effectively. With Gen Z's affinity for digital tools, using sophisticated gamification software allows for the seamless integration of gaming mechanics into the digital platforms they engage with daily. From gamified learning modules to productivity apps with gamification elements, the technology chosen must be intuitive, engaging, and capable of providing a rewarding experience.

However, gamification is not without its pitfalls. It's important to avoid overcomplication, which could lead to confusion or fatigue. The challenge is to strike the right balance between simplicity and depth, ensuring that the mechanics are easy to grasp but complex enough to remain interesting over time. Moreover, gamification requires careful design to avoid unintended consequences, such as fostering negative competition or overshadowing the non-gamified aspects of work that remain crucial.

The sustainability of gamification initiatives is another concern. It's not enough to create a one-time engagement boost. The gamification strategies must be dynamic, evolving with employees as they grow and the organization changes. Maintaining interest requires regularly updating challenges, rewards, and goals in line with both company direction and employee feedback.

Finally, privacy and data security are imperative when incorporating gamification. With Gen Z being highly conscious of their digital footprint, any gamification tools must be transparent in how they collect and use employee data. Assurance of data protection can prevent resentment and mistrust that could undermine the benefits of gamification.

In conclusion, gamification holds immense potential for motivating Gen Z employees, blending the lines between work and play. It can inspire enthusiasm, boost productivity, and enhance job satisfaction. Nevertheless, for gamification to be a powerful motivational tool, it must be thoughtfully crafted with the unique characteristics and expectations of Gen Z firmly in mind. A personalised, value-driven, and dynamic approach, which celebrates both individual and team achievements while fostering a deeper connection to the company's mission, is the cornerstone of successful gamification within the modern workplace.

Chapter 11: Financial Acumen and Compensation Models

In traversing from the engaging realms of communication and culture into the concrete stratifications of financial literacy and remuneration frameworks, understanding how to align fiscal incentives with the unique values of Generation Z becomes paramount. As we scrutinise financial acumen and compensation models, we peer into the aspirational dreams that animate this generation, appreciating their yen for transparency, fairness, and reward systems that echo their social and environmental consciousness. Modern compensation models must not only be robust and competitive but should also reflect a genuine resonance with the worldviews and desired impact of these emerging professionals. With a keen eye for innovation, Gen Z's compensation is more than just a paycheck; it's a mosaic of traditional monetary benefits, flexible perks, and opportunities for personal and professional growth that collectively inspire loyalty and drive performance. Aligning rewards with Gen Z's aspirations demands that HR leaders and organisational strategists develop an intuitive grasp of the nuanced interplay between meaningful work, societal contribution, and financial satisfaction, thus creating a blueprint for a future-ready business environment where mutual prosperity is the norm.

Aligning Values with Rewards

In the calculus of compensation, where numbers often speak louder than words, presenting rewards that resonate with Gen Z's intrinsic values becomes essential. This generation seeks to intertwine their personal ethos with their professional aspirations, pushing leaders to devise compensation models which do more than just dispense paychecks. They want a reward system that mirrors their commitment to sustainability, social impact, and ethical practices. Tailoring compensation to fit their aspirational goals, such as offering shares in a company with a vigorous CSR program or bonuses tied to environmental achievements, speaks their language. Aligning fiscal endowments with Gen Z's values not only garners their respect but also stimulates a higher level of performance, loyalty, and satisfaction, creating a symbiotic ecosystem where profit and purpose coexist seamlessly.

Understanding the Aspirational Goals of Gen Z

As the baton passes from Millennials, Generation Z emerges with a different set of goals, drives, and expectations that significantly colour their perceptions of work and life. Deeply committed to authenticity and led by a strong sense of individuality, Gen Z's aspirational goals challenge conventional norms and set new paradigms for what they perceive as meaningful work.

In a world teeming with global challenges – from climate change to socio-economic disparities – Gen Zers aspire to play an active role in crafting solutions. Their goals aren't just about securing a job; it's about aligning with organizations that reflect their values. They seek employment that allows them to contribute to the social good, prioritizing a sense of purpose over traditional markers of success such as job title or salary alone.

There's a vibrant entrepreneurial spirit within Gen Z. Their digital fluency has seen them grow up with boundless information and tools at their fingertips, instilling a strong belief in self-efficacy and the possibility of change. In the workplace, this tribe is looking for roles that offer autonomy, encourage innovation, and recognize their contributions through meaningful opportunities and projects.

Authenticity isn't just a buzzword for this generation; it's integral to how they navigate the world. They seek transparent work cultures where open conversations about goals, expectations, and feedback are the norm. The rigidity of hierarchical corporate structures is less appealing, as they favour environments that promote diverse perspectives and equitability.

For Gen Z, connectivity and tech-savvy are innate traits. More than any generation before, they expect their workplaces to employ advanced technologies not just for efficiency but for fostering collaboration and personal growth. Their comfort with an array of digital tools opens avenues for innovative problem-solving and agility within organizations.

Living through an era of significant activist movements, Gen Z's goals often include driving social change. They're inclined to contribute to organizations that not only speak on important issues but back their words with action. Companies committed to ethical practices and sustainability hold a particular allure, as this aligns with the generation's desire for impactful work.

Fulfillment for Gen Z goes beyond what happens in the office. They view their careers as part of a larger life picture, which includes wellbeing, community, and personal passions. The conventional separation of work and life is a less accepted concept, as they strive for a seamless integration that supports their overall quality of life.

Gen Z's approach to their careers is anything but linear. They view life as a series of experiences and are eager to gather a diverse range of them. This might involve pivoting between roles and industries or seeking out unconventional career paths that allow for personal exploration and skills development.

Financial stability is, understandably, another goal; however, it is often framed within the broader context of flexibility and mobility. Gen Zers value opportunities to learn and grow financially, such as through comprehensive benefits packages, investments in personal and professional development, and fair compensation frameworks reflecting their contribution and living costs.

Amid aspirations for global change and innovation, this generation hasn't lost sight of the importance of individual mental health and emotional intelligence. They aspire to roles and workplaces that not only acknowledge but actively support mental health, reflecting acknowledgment of its importance to overall productivity and satisfaction.

The dialogue surrounding diversity and inclusivity is one Gen Z is intimately familiar with. As digital citizens with access to a global community, they expect their workplaces to mirror this diversity. Their goals are geared towards contributing to organizations where inclusivity is not just a policy but practiced every day.

Education and continuous learning are central goals as well. Gen Z is the most educated generation to enter the workforce yet, and they have an appetite for learning that extends beyond formal education. They value the ability to upskill within their roles and appreciate employers who invest in learning and development.

Leadership is not about titles for Gen Z. They aspire to be part of flat, dynamic teams where everyone can lead in their areas of expertise. Leadership goals are centered around collaboration rather than command, and they are inclined towards mentorship programs that help them connect with experienced professionals.

In conclusion, Gen Z's aspirational goals pivot on the axes of authenticity, flexibility, technological integration, social responsibility, and continuous personal growth. For forward-thinking organisations, understanding these goals isn't just about attracting this generational cohort; it's also central to nurturing an innovative, inclusive, and future-focused business ethos.

As we continue to delve deeper into what makes Gen Z tick, it's evident that aligning organizational practices with their aspirations is not just advantageous – it's crucial. Gen Z is not just preparing to enter our workplaces; they are already here, and they're ready to redefine success and purpose in the business world.

Chapter 12: Health and Wellbeing in the Modern Office

Moving beyond traditional notions of wellness, forward-looking businesses are now focusing on the broader concept of wellbeing, encompassing mental, emotional, and physical health in the context of work. The integration of Generation Z into the workplace brings to the fore the importance of designing an office that's not just a place to work, but a space that supports the highest standards of health and wellbeing. This chapter delves into the imperative of cultivating an environment that prioritises mindfulness, resilience, and work-life integration—an approach that's instrumental in fostering a culture where young, dynamic workers feel valued and understood. Acknowledging that long hours and constant connectivity can lead to burnout, especially among the tech-savvy yet work-life conscious Gen Z, innovative office wellness programs are no longer optional but a vital aspect of organisational strategy. The modern office thus emerges as a crucible for wellbeing, buttressing not only the company's health but also its competitive edge in attracting and retaining the bright, motivated minds that drive success in the contemporary business landscape.

Mental Health and Emotional Intelligence

Perhaps one of the most compelling evolutions in the modern workplace centres around the importance placed on mental health and emotional intelligence – a trend that aligns well with the ethos of Generation Z employees. The convergence of these elements in today's office architecture doesn't merely spotlight an organisational shift; it encapsulates a grander societal awakening.

Emotional intelligence, a term popularised by psychologist Daniel Goleman, encapsulates the ability to understand and manage one's own emotions, as well as to recognise and influence the emotions of those around us. It's a cornerstone of effective team dynamics and leadership, and it's revered in contemporary work cultures for a good reason.

The modern office pulsates with diverse personalities and expectations, oft-times leading to complex emotional undercurrents. Generation Z brings to the table a heightened sense of emotional acuity, having grown up in an age where discussions on mental health are not eschewed but encouraged. Therefore, tapping into this generation's inherently keen emotional intelligence is vital for organisations aspiring to forge robust and empathetic teams.

Until recent times, business leaders have been lauded for their strategic acumen and unwavering decision-making. Yet, the tide is changing. Leaders are now expected to be adroit in the delicate art of emotional navigation. They must be equipped to handle stress, empathise with employees, and foster a supportive atmosphere that bolsters mental wellness.

Gen Z's entrance into the workforce comes at a time when the stigmas surrounding mental health are being dismantled. They seek employers who don't just pay lip service to mental wellness but those who embed support and mindfulness into the fabric of their corporate culture.

Forward-thinking organisations have made it a priority to engineer workspaces and regimes that uplift mental health. This encompasses stress-reduction programs, promoting physical activity, offering flexible work arrangements, and implementing open-door policies for discussions around mental wellbeing.

In the process, it's become clear that there's a symbiotic relationship between emotional intelligence and mental health. When team members are more emotionally intelligent, they're not only better equipped to handle their own stresses but also more attuned to the needs of their colleagues, creating a mutually supportive environment.

Integral to the modern office ethos is the concept of psychological safety – a term coined by organisational behavioural scientist Amy Edmondson, which denotes an environment where employees feel safe to express ideas, admit mistakes, and voice concerns without fear of reprisal. Building an emotionally intelligent workforce is key to creating such an environment.

The benefits of emotional intelligence extend beyond the office environment; they impinge positively on customer interactions, vendor negotiations, and stakeholder engagements. Employees adept at discerning emotional climates can pivot more effectively during negotiations, tailor their approach to client presentations, and build more robust relationships that fuel business growth.

Research suggests that teams with high levels of emotional intelligence are more productive, more profitable, and report higher levels of employee engagement. There is a clear business case for integrating training that enhances emotional intelligence into Gen Z-focused development programs.

Furthermore, it is essential to recognise that aerating the conversation around mental health isn't solely the preserve of human resources. It's a holistic commitment that emboldens every stratum of the organisation – from junior team members right up to C-suite executives. Leaders must lead by example, openly sharing and encouraging dialogue around mental health challenges and solutions.

Another essential facet of emotional intelligence is resilience – the ability to rebound from setbacks with poise and determination. This quality plays a pivotal role in maintaining mental health in the face of professional pressures. Offering workshops and resources on building resilience can arm employees, particularly Gen Z, with the fortitude to navigate through their burgeoning careers confidently.

To ignore the mental well-being of the workforce is to hobble the organisation's potential. Fostering emotional intelligence and caring for mental health isn't merely a 'nice-to-have' – it's a strategic imperative that can galvanise innovation, fortify corporate reputations, and engender a sustainable, high-performing organisational culture.

As we propel further into a landscape also shaped by Generation Z, the contouring of emotional intelligence and mental health care within the office environment won't just be seen as progressive; it will be the benchmark for any organisation that dares to claim it's at the vanguard of workplace evolution.

Ultimately, embracing emotional intelligence in support of mental health is not a one-off project but an enduring commitment. An organisation that prioritises these aspects will not only be an attractive prospect for Gen Z talent but will also set itself apart as a bastion of progressive workplace culture, ready to face the multifarious demands of the evolving business world.

Work-Life Integration Over Balance

In the grand tapestry of modern office life, the pursuit of health and wellbeing has transcended beyond physical wellness programs and ergonomic chairs. A new vista unfolds, beckoning a more holistic approach that entwines the very fibres of work and life into a seamless narrative. As leaders and strategists bespoke to the cause of harmonizing a workforce, we have observed that for Generation Z, the concept of work-life balance has metamorphosed into the ideal of work-life integration.

Traditional work setups, cleaving day from night and leisure from labour, have given way to an era where young employees anticipate fluidity and symbiosis between their jobs and personal lives. We are no longer seeing a quest for a perfect equilibrium; rather, an all-encompassing blend that regards work as a natural extension of life, and vice versa. This evolution has profound implications not just for the health and wellbeing of individuals, but for the operational strategies and cultural fabric of future-ready organisations.

To embrace work-life integration is to accept that Gen Z will check emails during dinner, but may also complete a personal online course during work hours. They will partake in a conference call from a café, followed by work on a passion project with the flexibility bestowed by remote working arrangements. This integration is not just a preference but a maxim of efficiency and self-fulfilment for the youngest cohort of our professional community.

Companies seeking to attract and retain talents of this generation must therefore recalibrate their policies, viewing workplace flexibility not as a perk, but as a non-negotiable cornerstone of their employee value proposition. Work from home, adaptable working hours, and the acceptance of the digital nomad lifestyle are becoming standard expectations that, if unmet, may send potential Gen Z powerhouses trotting to competitors.

Yet, this doesn't suggest an anarchical free-for-all devoid of structure. On the contrary, successful integration requires meticulous crafting of an environment that supports both autonomy and accountability. Tools and systems must be in place to enable seamless transitions between professional and personal tasks, ensuring that productivity is maintained without compromising wellbeing.

For instance, the introduction of project management software and communication platforms that can be accessed from any device plays a vital role. With these, Gen Z can collaborate with colleagues and manage their workloads effectively from any location or time zone, aligning their professional output with their personal lifecycles.

Furthermore, the traditional nine-to-five construct is being reshaped into condensed work weeks or split shifts, allowing for concentrated periods of work followed by extended periods for rest or personal endeavors. This is not only about giving employees control over their time but recognising that peak productivity does not fit neatly into eight-hour slots.

Integrating work and life also means extending the corporate support network to cover personal development and wellbeing. Enrichment workshops, mental health resources, and lifestyle benefits are invitingly woven into the company's culture, illustrating that an employee's value extends beyond mere output.

Leaders must be equipped to guide teams under this paradigm, evolving from supervisors of time to curators of experience. They must be more than managers; they should be mentors attuned to the rhythms of the individual, assisting in harmonizing the melody of work and life to help each team member thrive.

So, how do we measure success in this integrated environment? Traditional matrices like time spent in the office become obsolete, replaced by outcomes based evaluations. The focus shifts towards achieving goals, solving problems, and creating value, rather than merely clocking hours.

Addressing misgivings about potential abuses of this system is crucial, as trust is the currency of integration. Employers must believe in the commitment and self-discipline of their teams, while employees must exemplify integrity and professionalism across the blurred lines of work and personal domains. It's a mutual contract of respect and shared goals.

It is incumbent upon organisations to pilot programs that foster work-life integration, continuously testing and refining these initiatives. Employee feedback loops are indispensable in this process, ensuring that the needs and concerns of Gen Z are addressed, and that these programs enhance, rather than hinder, their passion and creativity.

Beyond the office walls, the reverberations of this shift touch the wider ecosystem of employment. Benefits packages and insurance offerings are adjusting to encompass the health impacts of this blend, recognising the individual as a whole, rather than as a segregated worker and personal entity.

In conclusion, work-life integration represents more than a fleeting trend—it signifies a pivotal transformation in organisational culture and personal wellbeing. For Gen Z, the harmonious blending of work and life experiences will not only shape their occupational landscape but define their contributions to society at large. It's a symphony where every note counts, an intricate dance of duty and delight that yields a richer, more nuanced performance of life's work.

As we progress through the labyrinth of change, remember: the future of work isn't waiting for us to catch up. Generation Z is already composing the score for the next movement—the wise among us will listen, learn, and lead the ensemble towards that integrated magnum opus.

Chapter 13:
Corporate Social Responsibility and Gen Z

As we delve into Chapter 13, we acknowledge the inextricable link between corporate social responsibility (CSR) and Gen Z's growing influence in the workforce. It has become increasingly clear that for businesses to attract, engage, and retain this cohort, they must embody values that resonate deeply with them. Gen Z isn't just looking for employment; they're seeking out organizations whose operations are steeped in ethical practices and community involvement. This chapter explores how aligning a company's mission with social, economic, and environmental stewardship can not only foster Gen Z loyalty but also elevate a brand's standing in the marketplace. We'll dissect how tapping into this generation's inherent drive for meaningful work can enable a symbiotic relationship where the pursuit of profit coexists with the quest to make a tangible positive impact on society.

Ethical Business Practices and Gen Z Loyalty

As we delve deeper into the topic of corporate social responsibility, it becomes increasingly apparent that ethical business practices are not merely a trend—they are a fundamental expectation from Generation Z. This cohort, having grown up in an era of instant access to information, is acutely aware of the societal and environmental footprints left by corporations. To retain loyalty among Gen Z employees, businesses must demonstrate a commitment to ethical standards that align with this generation's values.

Research suggests that ethical business practices resonate deeply with Gen Z. They tend to seek out employers with a strong ethical compass and are more likely to be loyal to companies that showcase integrity and social awareness. To them, actions speak louder than words, so it's imperative for companies to walk the talk when it comes to matters of ethics and responsibility.

The rationale behind Gen Z's attraction to ethical businesses lies in their worldview. They have inherited a range of social and environmental issues and feel a sense of urgency to address them. Companies that recognise their role in fostering positive change can capture the attention and dedication of this generation.

Transparency is a cornerstone of ethical business in the eyes of Gen Z. They expect honesty about how products are sourced, the labour practices involved in their creation, and the environmental impact of their production and distribution. Companies that provide this level of transparency are more likely to secure Gen Z's trust and loyalty.

Moreover, Gen Z values consistency across all touchpoints. A company that projects ethical practices in marketing but fails to embody them in its supply chain will quickly lose credibility with this generation. They are adept at uncovering discrepancies and will hold companies accountable for any gaps between their promotion and practice.

Corporate governance is another area closely scrutinised by Gen Z. They are inclined to work for and support businesses whose leaders demonstrate ethical decision-making and who cultivate an organisational culture grounded in fairness and ethical principles.

Inclusivity is not to be neglected when discussing ethics. Gen Z expects businesses to go beyond lip service, seeking genuine diversity and inclusivity within the workplace. They see this as a marker of ethical maturity, understanding that it contributes to better decision-making and a more humane, equitable world.

With regard to the environment, sustainable practices are a key marker of ethical business for Gen Z. They identify closely with companies that take proactive measures to minimise their environmental impact and contribute to sustainability goals. This dedication to eco-friendly operations is seen not just as corporate responsibility but as a defining character of a progressive, future-focused company.

Community involvement is another dimension where ethical practices can boost Gen Z loyalty. Companies that actively support local causes, engage in philanthropic activities, and contribute positively to community development will find a receptive audience among Gen Z. Their preference is for companies that act as good corporate citizens, enriching the spaces where they operate.

Social justice issues are also a priority for Gen Z. A company's commitment to fairness, equity, and justice in societal matters is a litmus test for many young employees and consumers. Companies that stand up for human rights and advocate for change can establish a deep sense of alignment with Gen Z values.

Furthermore, Gen Z is watching how companies handle data protection and privacy. In an age where personal information is frequently compromised, ethical handling of data is a significant concern. Companies that uphold high standards of data ethics and protect consumer and employee information can build a solid foundation of trust with this generation.

Product authenticity and integrity remain as crucial to Gen Z as the operations behind them. They favour products and services that are not only quality and sustainably made but that also resonate with their ethos. A company's product line, therefore, can be a reflection of its ethical stance and a magnet for Gen Z loyalty.

These various threads of ethical business—transparency, governance, inclusivity, sustainability, community involvement, social justice, and data ethics—are interwoven into the fabric of Gen Z's expectations. Businesses must understand that Gen Z loyalty is not simply secured through branding or one-off campaigns, but through consistent, authentic, and holistic ethical practices.

In conclusion, to garner the loyalty of Gen Z, it's not enough to simply appear ethical on the surface; companies must embody ethical principles through actionable initiatives and cultural ethos. Companies that integrate these practices into their core operations will not only thrive in terms of Gen Z loyalty but will also set new standards for what it means to conduct business responsibly in the modern world.

Community Engagement and Empowerment

When discussing the integration of Generation Z into the workforce, one can't overlook the importance of corporate social responsibility (CSR), specifically community engagement and empowerment. For organisations keen on harnessing the passion of Gen Z, it is essential to recognise that this demographic looks beyond the four walls of their workplace when it comes to their employer's ethical footprint. Gen Z's active interest in community involvement is a defining characteristic that employers should both appreciate and leverage.

This new wave of employees brings with it a heightened emphasis on direct impact. They are not only motivated by personal growth opportunities within an organisation but are also galvanised by projects that allow them to contribute to social causes. Companies wanting to attract and retain Gen Z talent should therefore place a significant emphasis on crafting and executing initiatives that support community development.

Empowerment goes hand in hand with engagement. To effectively engage with communities, businesses must offer more than charity; they must present opportunities for collaborative initiatives that empower community members to lead change. This could take numerous forms, such as supporting local entrepreneurship, providing educational workshops, or facilitating youth leadership programmes — areas where Gen Z's skill set can truly shine.

It's important to align CSR initiatives with the core values of an organisation, creating a natural synergy that resonates with Gen Z employees. When a company's community projects reflect its internal culture, it sends a powerful signal that the company lives by its values. This breeds a sense of authenticity that Generation Z values highly.

Furthermore, enabling Gen Z workers to have a say in community-related decisions not only leverages their intrinsic motivations but also fosters a sense of ownership and pride in their workplace. Gen Z is known for their desire to have a voice, and this approach makes room for their input, ensuring that empowerment is mutual — for the employees and the community.

Where traditional CSR initiatives may have leaned on a one-way relationship — company to community — inventive organisations are finding that a reciprocal relationship yields more meaningful results. Gen Z employees can benefit from community engagement by developing crucial skills such as leadership, problem-solving, and cross-cultural communication, which are honed when they tackle real-world issues.

Consider this — digital proficiency is an inherent trait of Gen Z. With their natural skill set, companies can empower communities by innovating digital literacy programmes where Gen Z professionals facilitate workshops. Such partnerships can open doors to new opportunities and foster a culture of digital inclusivity.

It's important to track and communicate the outcomes of these community engagements. When a company sets tangible goals and achieves measurable results, it not only reassures Gen Z employees of the integrity of their employer but it also sets a precedent for continuous improvement. Sharing these successes across the organisation and externally helps maintain momentum and showcases the company's commitment to social impact.

Moreover, such engagement and empowerment initiatives can evolve into long-term partnerships that benefit both the community and the company. By investing in communities, companies indirectly cultivate future talent pools and potential consumer bases — after all, Gen Z is deeply invested in the idea of growth alongside the communities they impact.

Transparency in these initiatives is key. Generation Z demands visibility into how their efforts, and those of their employer, are contributing to the greater good. This includes open dialogue about challenges faced and lessons learned, reinforcing the message that both success and setbacks are part of the journey towards positive change.

The leadership roles within these community initiatives should ideally be rotated, giving a diverse range of Gen Z employees the chance to lead. This not only equips them with vital experience but also showcases the organisation's commitment to egalitarian leadership and professional development.

When it comes to community engagement and empowerment, it's not all about grand gestures. Companies that enable small-scale, localized efforts often find that these resonate deeply with employees. These efforts allow Gen Z individuals to connect with their immediate surroundings and witness the direct consequences of their actions.

In practice, the intersection of technology and social good is an area ripe for innovative CSR programmes. Leveraging Gen Z's technological savvy to create platforms or apps that address local issues can enact change and serve as an incubator for socially-conscious tech solutions.

The bottom line is that for any company targeting to mould a workforce that includes Gen Z talent, CSR initiatives that focus on community engagement and empowerment are no longer optional, they are essential. By recognising and enabling Gen Z's drive for social change, these young professionals can become ardent champions of their company's values and be integrally involved in driving the company's impact agenda.

As we proceed to the next chapters, which delve into diversity, inclusivity, and legal implications of working with Gen Z, keep in mind that the foundation of these topics often begins with how a company treats its people and extends its duties beyond profit — to the communities it serves.

Chapter 14:
Diversity and Inclusivity As Core Values

As we delve into Chapter 14, it's paramount to recognise that diversity and inclusivity aren't just buzzwords to attract the burgeoning Gen Z workforce; they're essential principles fueling a paradigm shift within forward-looking businesses. Adopting diversity and inclusivity as core values means going beyond mere token gestures. It's about engineering organisational ecosystems that celebrate each individual's unique contributions while ensuring unimpeded access to opportunities—eradicating the glass ceilings and invisible barriers that have historically disadvantaged minority groups. To sustain relevance and inspire true innovation, companies must embed these ideals into their DNA, create a nurturing environment where respect and belonging are unequivocal, and methodically dismantle biases within recruitment and career progression frameworks. This isn't simply a matter of corporate benevolence; it's a strategic imperative that catalyses creativity, propels competitive advantage, and resonates profoundly with Generation Z's vision of an equitable, just workplace.

Fostering an Environment of Respect and Belonging

In constructing a workplace where diversity and inclusivity take centre stage, it's vital to also foster an environment of respect and belonging. As we walk through the doors into this dialogue, the key question at hand is: how can we create a space where every member of the workforce feels valued and essential to the fabric of the organisation? In the pursuit of this goal, there are several pivotal steps to consider.

Firstly, establishing organisational values that align with respect and belonging must be a priority. These values should be more than just words on a page; they must permeate every process, interaction, and decision within the company. To this end, it's critical that leadership teams exemplify these values in their actions, setting a tone from the top that reverberates throughout all levels of the organisation.

Communication is the cornerstone upon which the perception of respect is built. Leaders must foster an open dialogue, inviting differing perspectives, and ensuring that their ears are tuned to the diverse voices within the organisation. Such a communication-based approach breaks down barriers and builds trust, a non-negotiable component in the foundations of a respectful and inclusive environment.

In the spirit of inclusivity, it's equally important to actively celebrate the diverse backgrounds of employees. This can be manifested through highlighting significant cultural events, sharing stories that showcase varied heritages, and acknowledging the unique contributions that each individual brings to the table.

Going beyond mere celebration, structural inclusion must also be addressed. Policies and practices that support the various needs of employees must be deliberately crafted and implemented. This includes flexible working arrangements, equal opportunities for advancement, and providing necessary accommodations for individuals with disabilities.

Training plays a crucial role in nurturing a mindset of inclusivity and respect. Workshops and seminars that focus on unconscious bias, cultural competence, and inclusive leadership skills can arm employees with the tools they need to contribute to a welcoming workplace culture.

Safe and supportive reporting channels must be put in place to ensure that concerns regarding disrespect and exclusion can be raised without fear of retribution. Employees must feel assured that if they speak up, they will be heard and that appropriate action will be taken to address their concerns.

A sense of belonging can be particularly cultivated through mentoring and sponsorship programmes. By pairing employees with mentors, especially those from underrepresented groups, organisations can create powerful relationships that nurture professional growth and promote a sense of investment in every individual's success.

However, mentorship alone won't suffice. An organisation's commitment to advancement and leadership pathways for all employees, especially for those from marginalised groups, is a litmus test for its investment in respect and belonging.

Feedback mechanisms should be implemented where employees can regularly share their feelings and experiences regarding inclusion in the workplace. These insights can help leaders understand the effectiveness of current initiatives and identify areas requiring improvement.

Recognition of good practices connected to fostering an environment of respect is equally essential. When employees witness their colleagues being rewarded for inclusive behaviour, a positive reinforcement cycle begins, encouraging others to follow suit.

It's also critical to understand and support the individual life circumstances of each employee, promoting inclusivity beyond the workspace. Initiatives that support work-life integration, such as parental leave policies, childcare support, and attention to mental health, can create a profoundly positive impact on the sense of belonging for all employees.

Digital technology should also be leveraged to support inclusivity. With tools that enable collaboration and communication, remote team members feel more aligned with those in the office. This balance ensures that the camaraderie and connection aren't lost just because some team members work off-site.

Moreover, the physical workspace itself should reflect the organisation's commitment to inclusivity. Spaces designed to be accessible and comfortable for a diverse workforce, with consideration for different work styles and needs, mirror an organisation's respect for its employees.

It's not only about internal measures. Organisations must also consider the external impact of their inclusivity efforts. Establishing partnerships with diverse suppliers, engaging with local communities, and participating in initiatives that support equity and justice all contribute to a broader culture of respect and belonging.

Finally, measuring and reporting on diversity and inclusion efforts is indispensable. Organisational analytics should include metrics related to inclusion, respect, and belonging. These data points will not only track progress but also ensure accountability, driving continuous improvement in efforts to foster an inclusive culture.

As we look towards integrating Gen Z into our workspaces, it's clear that building an environment that resonates with respect and belonging is not just a moral imperative; it's a strategic necessity. Such an environment acts as a catalyst for creativity, innovation, and ultimately, the ongoing success of any forward-thinking business.

Inclusivity in Recruitment and Progression

As forward-leaning organizations continue to navigate the nuances of a diverse workforce, special attention must be given to inclusivity in recruitment and progression practices. It's in this aspect that one can distinguish a genuinely inclusive company from one merely playing lip service to diversity and inclusivity.

In the quest to attract Generation Z talent, inclusivity isn't just a policy tucked away in the employee handbook—it's an actionable response to the genuine concerns and aspirations of a new generation. When we speak of inclusivity, it encompasses a broad range of efforts—from ensuring a diverse pool of candidates to providing equitable access to growth opportunities within the company.

It starts with the recruitment process. Ads and job postings must be designed to appeal to a diverse demographic, free of gender-coded words and indicative of an environment that respects and thrives on diversity. Moreover, organizations can aim to remove bias by using software that blurs candidates' names and photos, thus focusing only on skills and capabilities.

During the interview stage, inclusivity means having a diverse panel of interviewers. A varied representation not only provides different perspectives but also signals to candidates that the company doesn't pay homage to homogeneity. Gen Z candidates are particularly observant of this; they often choose employers whose workforce reflects the world they live in.

But inclusivity shouldn't halt after the hiring process. It should seamlessly transition into thoughtful onboarding experiences that celebrate the unique backgrounds of new hires, offering them a sense of belonging from day one. Here, companies might implement mentorship programs that support professional development and foster inter-generational relationships.

Beyond onboarding, career progression for these fresh talents is where inclusivity takes on greater depth. The proverbial table at which decisions are made must reflect diverse opinions, experiences, and cultural backgrounds. It's about cultivating an atmosphere where Gen Z employees feel empowered to compete for promotions and leadership roles on an even playing field.

To facilitate this, transparent criteria for advancement and leadership pipelines that include individuals from underrepresented groups are critical. Practices such as open posting of all available positions and clear, consistently applied criteria for advancement send a powerful message that everyone has an equal shot at success.

An inclusive workplace also holds space for different styles of working and problem-solving. Accommodating varied work preferences is a vital piece of the puzzle for Generation Z, who have different expectations of work-life integration than previous generations.

Moreover, to truly advance inclusivity in progression, ongoing education on unconscious bias for all employees, including leadership, is vital. By addressing biases head-on, companies can ensure that all employees have the knowledge to support a fair and equitable work environment.

Inclusivity impacts retention as well. Organizations that continuously seek feedback from employees and adjust practices amid a backdrop of openness foster not just loyalty, but a culture where growth is nurtured. For Gen Z workers who value feedback and continuous improvement, this is a resonant approach.

One novel strategy companies can adopt is to create inclusion councils or committees dedicated to maintaining a focus on these core values. These groups can offer a platform for discussion, driving forward initiatives around recruitment and progression that reflect the values of inclusivity and diversity.

In essence, a diverse and inclusive company is one that mirrors the real world, respecting the richness of experiences Gen Z brings to the table. This generation isn't just looking for a job; they're seeking a workplace that respects their distinct perspectives and provides growth opportunities that don't have a glass ceiling.

Let's not forget that inclusivity also hinges on work-life integration. Parents, caregivers, and individuals with different abilities or health concerns must feel supported in their career journey. Flexible working arrangements, accessible workplace infrastructure, and empathetic leadership can greatly impact the sense of inclusion felt by employees.

To sum up, inclusivity is not a static goal but a dynamic journey that continues to evolve as organizations learn, grow, and adapt. Firms that embrace inclusivity, not only in their recruitment rhetoric but in concrete career progression practices, earn more than just profits—they garner the respect, devotion, and innovative spirit of a generation ready to define the future of work.

In conclusion, recruitment and progression policies that eloquently speak the language of inclusivity are not optional in the modern workplace—they are imperative for any business aiming to not only attract but also sustain Gen Z talent. For companies willing to embark on this journey, the rewards go beyond filling quotas or ticking boxes; they set a path toward a more holistic, equitable, and profitable future.

Chapter 15:
Legal Considerations and Compliance

Integrating Generation Z into the workplace not only demands adaptive strategies and dynamic leadership but also requires meticulous attention to the evolving legal landscape and compliance obligations that govern employment and data security. As we navigate the complexities of employment law with a demographic keen on transparency and ethics, it's paramount to understand that regulatory frameworks are constantly being updated to reflect the digital and diverse nature of the modern workforce. This chapter delves into the specific legal considerations companies must account for when onboarding Gen Z talent—from stringent data protection regulations to the nuances of employment contracts that speak to their desire for flexibility and work-life integration. Furthermore, as Gen Z brings a distinctive set of values and expectations, organisations must proactively align their practices with the latest laws to ensure they don't just avoid potential liabilities but also foster a culture of trust and respect, essential for attracting and retaining the brightest young minds. It's not just about ticking boxes; it's about building a legal framework that supports an innovative and inclusive future.

Navigating Employment Law with Gen Z

As business leaders and organisational architects, our quest to foster a dynamic workplace increasingly involves understanding the unique interplay between Generation Z and employment law. Indeed, our legal and compliance frameworks must adapt to the nuances of an emerging workforce that grew up against a backdrop of rapid technological evolution and shifting social paradigms.

When integrating Gen Z into our work environments, we confront an array of legal considerations that resonate with their distinct values. These include flexibility in work arrangements, inclusivity in employment practices, and a sharp emphasis on ethical standards in business dealings.

Youthful and informed, Gen Zers enter the workplace with an instinctive awareness of their rights and an expectation that their employers will not only comply with the law but will uphold high moral and ethical standards. This cognizance of legal entitlements extends to contracts, equal opportunity, and workplace safety, all of which are non-negotiable in their pursuit of employment. Hence, it's imperative for businesses to ensure their legal teams are attuned to these expectations.

With the growth of remote and flexible working arrangements, we now address an expanded view of employment law that encompasses this segment's desire for autonomy. However, it's not just about providing freedom; it's about mastering the legal intricacies of telecommuting policies, ergonomic and safe home office setups, and being mindful of work-life boundaries to prevent burnout.

Privacy is another key legal facet when dealing with Gen Z—a generation that values transparency, yet demands control over their personal data. Employers must navigate the tightrope between leveraging employee data for productivity and respecting the legal bounds of privacy. This means understanding and operating within the stringent requirements of data protection laws such as the GDPR (General Data Protection Regulation).

Furthermore, alongside respecting privacy, there lies an obligation to guard against discrimination and foster inclusivity. Gen Z's strong commitment to diversity and equality means they expect organisations to transcend the minimum anti-discrimination laws. This anticipation extends to equitable hiring and promotion practices, ensuring that we aren't just compliant but are actively championing diverse workplaces.

Of particular importance is understanding the intersectionality between technology and the law. As digital natives, Gen Zers are not only adept in tech usage but also well-informed on legal issues related to cybersecurity risks and liabilities. Implementing robust IT policies and educating staff on cyber law will mitigate the risks associated with the use of technology in business processes.

The gig economy has also shaped Gen Z's view on employment, with many leaning towards freelance and contract work. With that in mind, it's critical to draft clear contractual agreements that acknowledge the fluidity of modern work engagements while maintaining compliance with employment laws. These agreements should reflect fair compensation, delineate IP ownership, and detail dispute resolution protocols.

When it comes to individual wellbeing, mental health provisions are no longer optional. It's a legal requirement in many jurisdictions to ensure the workplace does not harm an employee's mental health. A Gen Z-attuned HR policy must include the promotion of mental health awareness, the provision of appropriate support structures, and the mitigation of workplace stressors.

Gen Z's environmental consciousness requires businesses to align their operations with sustainable practices. This is not only an ethical demand but often a legal one, as environmental laws become increasingly stringent. Organisations that acknowledge these expectations through policies and practices can avoid legal pitfalls and simultaneously attract Gen Z talent.

Training and development represent key facets of Gen Z's expectations. Employers should thus focus on crafting learning and growth opportunities within the legal remit of educational incentives. This may require navigating tax implications and ensuring that any educational benefits comply with both national and local educational laws.

In the wake of #MeToo and other social movements, workplace harassment and bullying laws have become a focal point for compliance. Gen Z employees expect their employers to go beyond compliance by creating a culture that actively prevents harassment. Proactive education and stringent anti-harassment policies must form the backbone of a respectful workplace.

Lastly, in preparation for the inevitable evolution of the workforce, being proactive about employment law compliance isn't just good ethics—it's strategic business sense. Up-to-date employment policies and regular legal audits can safeguard against potential litigation and boost organisational credibility among discerning Gen Z employees.

Understanding and navigating the multifaceted domain of employment law with respect to Gen Z is not only about avoiding legal jeopardy. It's about embodying best practices that resonate with a generation that is ethically driven and legally savvy. To thrive in this modern landscape, it's essential that businesses are not merely observers of legal changes but proactive participants in crafting an equitable and law-abiding workplace culture.

In sum, as leaders, our commitment to upholding and advancing the legal rights and privileges of Gen Z will indubitably be a testament to our business' values and our dedication to sustaining a workplace that's not only compliant but also conscientious and forward-thinking. Through astute legal navigation, we can unlock the full potential of

Gen Z and ensure a resilient and innovative future for our organisations.

Data Protection and Regulatory Challenges

As businesses eagerly integrate Generation Z talents into their workforce, they must navigate an evolving labyrinth of data protection and regulatory challenges. These novices in the workforce, born and bred in an era of unparalleled digital connectivity, bring with them a heightened expectation of privacy and data security.

Understanding this salient generational attribute means recognising that data protection is not merely a legislative hurdle, but a pivotal aspect of organisational integrity that Gen Z values profoundly. Generation Z's inherent digital savviness is twofold; it can be a boon to innovation but also introduces a myriad of vulnerabilities that companies must safeguard against.

Moving forward, companies should be acutely aware of the legislative landscape surrounding data privacy. The EU's General Data Protection Regulation (GDPR) and similar laws elsewhere set a high standard, serving as a testament to the global shift towards more robust data protection measures. These regulations present a gauntlet of compliance obligations, from the handling of personal data to its portability and the right to be forgotten.

For organisations, this involves meticulous data mapping and governance processes that might seem formidable at first blush. A Gen Z-inclusive workplace must foster a culture where data privacy is engrained in every process, with protocols duly documented and accessible. Regular training sessions and the integration of privacy by design principles into all systems and operations are not just regulatory requirements; they are a language that Gen Z speaks and appreciates.

It's also critical for leaders to collaborate with legal and IT teams to anticipate the impact of emerging technologies. As businesses continue to adopt AI, machine learning, and other advanced data-processing tools to attract this generation's talent, they inadvertently encounter the spectre of bias, misuse, and increased scrutiny from regulators.

To tackle these nuances, a Handbook of Data Ethics may be cultivated, merging legalese with the vernacular of technological innovations. Such a manual would go beyond legal requirements and address ethical considerations, resonating with the moral compass that guides the Gen Z mindset.

Regarding legal compliance, businesses must recognise that Generation Z is not a homogenous block. As the most socially aware generation to date, Gen Z's stance on privacy issues often dovetails with that of activist groups and watchdog agencies. This convergence means companies can no longer afford a reactive stance to regulatory changes. They must anticipate shifts and be at the vanguard of adopting best practices.

It's also pertinent to recognise that as digital natives, Gen Z members are particularly adept at using digital platforms for self-expression. They expect not just transparency but a voice in dialogues about their data. This necessitates systems that enable consent to be more dynamic and involvement in how their personal data is wielded.

Bridging this expectation requires a nimble but principled approach. Organisations should foster a two-way conversation on privacy matters by establishing channels for Gen Z employees to voice concerns and contribute to policy development. Data protection can't be an edict from on high; it must be a collective, ongoing conversation that champions individual autonomy.

As global citizens, many Gen Z employees also bring an international perspective to privacy. Thus, businesses must consider cross-border data transfer mechanisms and international compliance regulations. They must tread carefully, balancing the sanctity of data protection with the fluidity that globalized teams necessitate.

In this regard, Data Protection Officers (DPOs) become pivotal, serving as both the commanders and connectors in the compliance matrix. Their role extends beyond traditional compliance checkboxes; they must be educators, advocates, and strategists in an environment where each Gen Z talent might wield their data trail like a tapestry of their personal and professional ethos.

Another dimension to consider is the proliferation of personal devices and Bring Your Own Device (BYOD) policies within the workplace. Generation Z employees often juggle multiple personal devices, all of which could pose a threat to organisational data security if not managed correctly. It is vital to implement robust cybersecurity policies that align with BYOD trends, ensuring secure access to company networks and safeguarding sensitive information.

Moreover, with Gen Z being especially active online, companies must also navigate the capricious terrain of social media. Engaging this tech-savvy generation means crafting social media guidelines that enable self-expression while minimising legal and reputational risks.

Amidst this assemblage of challenges, a forward-looking enterprise will not only comply with regulation but will champion data stewardship as a cornerstone of their organisational ethos. They will use their robust data governance frameworks not as shackles but as scaffolds upon which trust and loyalty with Generation Z are built.

Finally, as companies diligently work to amalgamate Gen Z's proclivities with statutory requirements, they are drafting the next chapter of the corporate saga—a narrative where reverence for individual data rights and integrity is as integral to business success as the bottom line. Compliance with data protection regulations, when performed with a genuine commitment to privacy, becomes a differentiator in attracting and retaining the brightest minds of a generation that is inherently wary of the digital landscape's pitfalls.

Chapter 16:
Nurturing Entrepreneurial Traits
Within Corporates

Embracing the notion that the future of innovation lies within the energetic cadence of Gen Z's entrepreneurial spirit, corporates can prime themselves for an era of unbounded growth and competitive agility. By sculpting an environment that not only permits but actively encourages side hustles, corporates might witness a surge in innovative thinking and problem-solving prowess. You'll find that the most dynamic intrapreneurship programmes are those that function as a sandbox for this new generation to meld their technological savvy with a daring approach to business. These workshops, blended with a corporate culture that symbolises fearlessness in the face of new ventures, have been shown to instill a sense of ownership and drive amongst young professionals. It isn't merely about allowing Gen Z to explore entrepreneurial ventures within the firm's context; it's about fostering a hotbed of creative thinking that could incubate the next revolutionary product or service. This chapter is an expedition into the heart of creating a corporate ethos that doesn't just accommodate, but wholeheartedly embraces and cultivates, the natural entrepreneurial inclinations of a generation poised to disrupt industries and spearhead innovation.

Encouraging Side Hustles and Innovation

The entrepreneurial spirit is one that redefines conventional wisdom, pushing boundaries and fostering an environment where creativity thrives. To nurture this in a corporate setting, we must not only allow but encourage the pursuit of side hustles and personal innovation projects. In the age of Generation Z—the cohort that's set to reshape our workplace—this encouragement isn't simply nice to have; it's essential for the longevity and adaptability of an organisation.

Side hustles, often a byproduct of personal passion or a drive to solve real-world problems, can serve as a powerful catalyst for innovation. They enable employees to develop new skills, explore emerging markets, and test radical ideas outside the scope of their primary job functions. Moreover, these ventures often inspire an entrepreneurial mindset that can translate to increased initiative and problem-solving abilities within the corporate sphere.

For many in Gen Z, job security stems from their ability to pivot and adapt, rather than from longstanding loyalty to one company. They see side hustles not only as a method to generate supplementary income but as incubators for their aspirations. Their fluid approach to career development is one where agility takes precedence, with multiple interests explored in parallel to their main employment.

Companies stand to gain significantly by acknowledging and supporting their employees' entrepreneurial ambitions. By providing platforms that encourage the sharing of ideas cultivated in their personal projects, businesses can tap into a wealth of innovation that might otherwise remain siloed. This symbiotic relationship can enhance corporate agility and foster a shared sense of purpose and contribution.

It's crucial to create clear policies that delineate the boundaries between employees' independent ventures and their work for the company, ensuring that conflict of interests is preemptively addressed. Transparency and open communication about side ventures can mitigate potential risks while strengthening trust between employees and management.

Supportive measures could entail flexible working arrangements, allowing employees to better manage their time across various commitments. Allocation of 'innovation time' during the work week, similar to practices at forward-thinking tech firms, could provide structured opportunities for employees to focus on personal development and innovation that could benefit the firm.

Encouraging collaboration between employees on their personal projects within the corporate ecosystem can create dynamic cross-pollination of ideas. What's more, fostering an extensive internal network for sharing insights and resources can help to ignite collective creativity and accelerate the innovation process.

The influx of Gen Z into the workforce brings with it a digital savvy and a native approach to technology that can immensely benefit corporates. Harnessing their proficiency with digital tools and platforms enables companies to streamline processes and develop new solutions. When given the freedom to innovate, Gen Z can offer fresh perspectives on how to integrate these tools into the company's operations and strategy.

Mentoring programs that pair seasoned executives with young entrepreneurs can facilitate knowledge exchange and provide guidance. Experienced professionals can offer insights into navigating corporate structures, while the younger generation can share trends and novel approaches that may be off the radar of their seasoned counterparts.

Competitions or hackathons that challenge employees to develop solutions for company-specific issues can also stimulate intrapreneurship. Recognising and rewarding employees whose side projects contribute to the company's mission not only spurs further innovation but also enhances employee engagement and retention.

Hosting regular forums where employees can present their side projects and receive feedback fosters a culture of knowledge sharing and continuous learning. This practice celebrates the pursuit of side hustles openly, thereby stigmatizing the notion of 'moonlighting' in secret due to fear of reprisal or job loss.

Leveraging social intranet or innovation management platforms can help organisations track and manage the flow of ideas. These spaces can act as incubators for entrepreneurial projects, providing Gen Z employees with the resources and support they need to develop their ventures while remaining aligned with corporate goals.

It's not enough to simply allow for innovation to occur organically; active investment in employee growth paths that skew towards entrepreneurial skills will develop more resourceful and agile professionals. Investment can come in the form of funding, time allocation, or even access to the company's network. This not only benefits the budding entrepreneurs but also builds a reserve of talent poised to drive future corporate initiatives.

Ultimately, a culture that embraces side hustles and innovation as part of its fabric demonstrates a commitment to employee autonomy and development. By aligning corporate strategies with the entrepreneurial energy of Gen Z, companies can create an ecosystem where both the organisation and its employees are geared towards sustained innovation and growth.

By unlocking the potential within each employee to contribute transformative ideas and solutions, companies don't just keep up with the changing business landscape; they help to shape it. This culture of encouragement is not merely a trend to attract young talent—it's a strategic imperative in a world where adaptability and innovation are the currencies of success.

Intrapreneurship Programmes and Workshops

Progressive enterprises understand that the key to sustained innovation lies in leveraging the entrepreneurial traits within their talent pool. This is particularly essential in attracting, retaining, and nurturing Generation Z – a cohort renowned for their enterprising spirit. To foster this spirit within a structured corporate environment, it is crucial to implement intrapreneurship programmes and workshops, which serve as an incubator for entrepreneurial thinking and skills.

Intrapreneurship programmes are not just about inspiring creativity; they're about practical application and providing the resources necessary for employees to turn their innovative ideas into internal ventures. Corporates can offer structured workshops that equip young talent with the methodologies and tools of entrepreneurial success, meanwhile reinforcing the company's commitment to driving change from within.

These workshops aim to address several key areas: from ideation techniques to assessing market needs, from agile project management to iterative development. Tailoring these programmes to reflect current business challenges ensures relevance and immediate applicability, further stimulating the engagement of Gen Z professionals who seek purpose in their work.

Many Gen Z employees arrive with a digital-first mindset that should be harnessed and directed through these programmes. Workshops on digital entrepreneurship, therefore, do not only touch upon current digital tools and platforms but also on emerging technologies, preparing the workforce for the continual evolution of the digital landscape and maintaining a competitive edge.

Another crucial theme within intrapreneurship workshops is to offer guidance on how to build resilient business models that withstand market fluctuations. Learning from failed initiatives is an integral part of entrepreneurial growth, and such programmes should encourage participants to adopt a fail-fast, learn-quickly mentality.

This approach condones healthy risk-taking and continuous improvement – attributes that Generation Z admires.

While technical skills and business acumen form the backbone of these workshops, it's vital not to overlook the human element – nurturing leadership capabilities, teamwork, and negotiation skills. These workshops create platforms for cross-departmental collaboration, where individuals from various functions can partner, exchange ideas, and build on each other's strengths.

Mentorship, too, plays a pivotal role in the success of intrapreneurial ventures. Pairing young intrapreneurs with seasoned executives can ignite powerful synergies, transferring knowledge while challenging established norms. This cross-pollination enriches the company's culture and injects new perspectives into the upper echelons of management.

Setting up internal 'innovation labs' or 'hackathons' as part of these programmes offers a palpable excitement to the corporate routine, which resonates with the interactive and challenge-seeking nature of Gen Z. These events also present tangible outcomes, which is a significant motivator for this results-oriented generation. A culture of recognition and reward for innovative solutions enhances motivation and creates a sense of accomplishment.

However, to ensure these programmes thrive, leadership must demonstrate genuine support. A clear pathway for the implementation of successful projects to be rolled out at a corporate level must exist. Transparent communication on how ideas are evaluated and decisions made is crucial for maintaining trust and continued involvement.

Metrics are equally essential. Establishing key performance indicators (KPIs) for intrapreneurship initiatives helps quantify their impact and importance to the business overall. Success can be measured in patent filings, prototype developments, or even efficiency savings – all contributing to a narrative of growth propelled by internal entrepreneurialism.

As businesses progressively internationalise their operations, intrapreneurship workshops need to integrate cross-cultural intelligence as well. It's pivotal for upcoming intrapreneurs to understand and navigate the complexities of global marketplaces, considering the diverse socio-economic conditions and business etiquettes.

On the horizon are more developments focusing on sustainability, given Gen Z's affinity for social and environmental responsibility. Intrapreneurial programmes can incorporate sustainability-driven innovation, combining corporate growth with positive societal impact – thus reinforcing the notion of ethical profitability.

In conclusion, by prioritizing intrapreneurship programmes and workshops, companies can create an environment that not only delights and retains Generation Z talent but also serves as a catalyst for continuous corporate rejuvenation. These programmes are the playgrounds where young visionaries can experiment, fail, learn, and ultimately drive forward the innovative agenda that will shape our common future.

Chapter 17:
Preparing Leaders for a Gen Z Workforce

As we pivot from the ambitious entrepreneurial frameworks discussed in Chapter 16, it's imperative that we focus on tailoring leadership development for a vibrant Gen Z workforce. In a landscape where traditional hierarchies are challenged, leaders are required to foster environments that thrive on innovation, responsiveness, and a genuine commitment to social values. Cultivating such a climate means that executives must not only equip themselves with an intimate understanding of Gen Z's unique motivations but also undergo a transformation in their approach to mentorship, decision-making, and communication. Adapting to the expectations of younger leaders involves reimagining conventional strategies to resonate with a generation that prizes authenticity, technological fluency, and purpose above all else. To seize this opportunity, organisations stand at the precipice of a crucial evolution, one that demands that senior leaders become adept at navigating the nuances of Generation Z's work ethic and aspirations, ensuring that the transfer of the leadership baton is as seamless as it's revolutionary.

Leadership Development and Succession Planning

As businesses move steadfastly into the future, it is pivotal to mould leaders who are not merely astute decision-makers but agile mentors, adept at navigating the intricacies of a Gen Z-dominated workforce. Leadership development and succession planning become critical components in this terrain, demanding attention from those at the helm.

The crux of developing leaders for such a highly discerning and progressive cohort lies not just in technical training, but in cultivating a leadership philosophy that resonates with Gen Z's value system. These emerging leaders must emphasize inclusivity, foster a culture of continuous learning and advocate for innovation and creativity as part of their modus operandi.

Integrating Gen Z into high-level strategic planning signifies a shift in traditional succession planning. Just as this generation is driven by a desire for accelerated career progression, so must the pathways to leadership be responsive and fluid, enabling young talent to visualize their potential ascent within a company.

To cultivate a robust pipeline of future leaders, it's essential that organisations harness not only the strengths of Gen Z but also the collaborative wisdom of multi-generational teams. Through cross-generational mentoring programs, seasoned professionals can pass on their insights, while simultaneously gleaning fresh perspectives from their younger colleagues.

However, mentorship alone is not sufficient. A rich tapestry of learning and development opportunities must be weaved, characterised by both online and offline experiences. Microlearning modules, hackathons, and innovation labs become indispensable in this learning ecosystem, all strategically aligned with Gen Z's aptitude for digital environments and their inclination towards social learning.

Identifying potential leaders within Gen Z also requires new approaches. Look for those who exhibit a sense of ownership and engagement in projects beyond their scope, those who can navigate ambiguity with a poised resolve. This entrepreneurial spirit, coupled with a strong ethical compass, often marks those ready for elevation.

Forward-thinking enterprises must break away from rigid, linear succession plans and embrace adaptable grids of roles and experiences. This approach resonates with Gen Z's preference for non-hierarchical organisation structures and their ambition to partake in various aspects of the business, which encourages a holistic understanding of the company's operations.

Supporting this fluidity, technology becomes an enabler for leadership training. Through virtual reality scenarios, AI-driven simulations, and remote coaching platforms, organisations can create immersive experiences that challenge Gen Z employees in safe but realistic environments.

Leadership development for Gen Z also beckons a departure from an 'all work, no play' approach, ushering in methodologies that incorporate elements of gamification. This not only bolsters engagement but allows for the development of strategic thinking and problem-solving skills in a manner akin to their interactions outside of work.

Succession planning for a Gen Z workforce further stipulates a transparent and inclusive process. Dialogues around succession must be consistent and open, ensuring that everyone has access to the same information and opportunity for advancement, regardless of background, thus reinforcing an ethos of meritocracy.

A critical aspect of readying leaders for this cohort is nurturing emotional intelligence. The modern leader must be adept at understanding and managing not only their own emotions but those of others, fostering a work environment where mental health is prioritised, and resilience is built.

Moreover, contemporary leadership development programs must emphasise sustainability—not as a peripheral consideration but as a core leadership responsibility. The future leader must be equipped to integrate sustainable practices into the company's strategy, reflecting Gen Z's strong environmental conscience.

This forward-thinking approach to leadership development and succession planning does not merely prime an organisation for an immediate influx of Gen Z talent. It also sets a precedent for ongoing organisational evolution, creating an infrastructure that is perpetually future-ready and adaptable to the nuances of ensuing generations.

To that end, organisations must institute regular reviews of their leadership development and succession planning strategies. The dynamic nature of the workforce, amplified by the ever-evolving landscape of technological advancements, mandates a continuous re-evaluation to ensure alignment with not only the expectations of Gen Z but the future that lies beyond.

In conclusion, organisations must act with intention and agility to build a leadership cadre that can connect with, inspire, and lead a Gen Z workforce. Hand in hand with Gen Z, these leaders will forge a burgeoning legacy of innovation, diversity, and sustainability, hallmarks of the modern workplace that together, they will create and navigate.

Adapting to the Expectations of Younger Leaders

As we move deeper into the 21st century, a wave of change has begun to ripple through our organisational structures and leadership models. This wave is being propelled by Generation Z, who are not merely content with filling roles but are keen to reshape them. Leaders and managers must recognise that these younger individuals often view leadership through a different lens, one that invites collaboration, innovation, and a flatter hierarchy. Adapting to their expectations is essential for companies that strive to remain relevant and forward-thinking in an evolving corporate landscape.

The traditional top-down leadership approach no longer resonates with Gen Z, who have grown up in a world where information, mentorship, and feedback flow freely through digital channels. They expect a similar structure in their professional lives, one that encourages dialogue, openness, and a shared vision. This necessitates a transformation in leadership styles; to foster an environment where young leaders feel empowered, engaged, and integral to decision-making processes.

For these digital natives, innovation isn't just welcomed; it's expected. Leaders of tomorrow must thus learn to not only accept but to drive and manage change whilst maintaining an eye on the stability of the organisation. Facilitating a culture where trial and error are viewed as stepping stones to success will harmonise with Gen Z's perception of progress. This requires fostering an environment that values creativity and offers leeway for young leaders to experiment and take calculated risks without the fear of reprisal.

Moreover, younger leaders have grown up in a deeply interconnected world and so have a natural inclination towards global thinking and inclusivity. They're likely to challenge the status quo by demanding workplaces that are more diverse and inclusive. In response, leadership must exemplify these qualities, actively work to break down barriers, and create pathways for diverse voices to influence company strategy and culture.

The role of technology in shaping expectations is also pivotal. Gen Z leaders have innate technological prowess and will seek out companies that leverage technology not just for the sake of digitisation but for the enhancement of productivity, collaboration, and employee wellbeing. Thus, leaders must embrace and adapt to cutting-edge tools and platforms to maintain synchronicity with their younger counterparts.

Young leaders show a pronounced preference for social responsibility and meaningful work. Hence, companies aiming to attract and retain this cohort of the workforce must align their values and business practices with social and environmental responsibility. Leaders that can credibly integrate and advocate for these values within corporate strategies will gain the respect and commitment of Gen Z professionals.

Communication styles are shifting as well. Gen Z favours authentic and transparent interaction, which breaks down the walls of formality that traditionally exist between different levels of hierarchy. For more seasoned leaders, this means learning to communicate in a relatable manner—swapping corporate jargon for clear, concise, and genuine dialogue.

Feedback and mentorship are core expectations for young leaders who often seek continuous learning and growth opportunities. It's incumbent upon established leaders to become proficient mentors and build a framework for ongoing professional development. An effective leader will proactively offer guidance and support, recognising that the growth of their Gen Z colleagues directly correlates with the advancement of the organisation.

Leaders must cultivate agility to meet the flexibility demanded in modern work environments. Gen Z professionals are proponents of remote working, flexible hours, and project-based roles, showing less interest in the traditional 9-to-5 confines. Successfully adapting to this will involve reshaping policies and measuring performance based on output and innovation rather than time spent at a desk.

The aspiration for work-life integration is a further consideration that can't be downplayed. Younger leaders aren't interested in sacrificing personal time for corporate loyalty; they seek synergy between professional and personal lives. This will challenge leaders to devise roles and responsibilities in a manner that reflects this priority without compromising on productivity or business objectives.

Within this evolving paradigm, succession planning takes on a new perspective. Identifying and grooming young leaders must be an active and strategic process. Leadership development programmes should be tailored to the unique aptitudes and career aspirations of Gen Z, providing pathways for advancement that align with their diverse skills and ambitions.

Lastly, leaders will find that they are increasingly serving not only as managers but as facilitators of purpose-driven work. Gen Z is acutely motivated by purpose, often rating it as high as, if not higher than, financial compensation. Leadership then becomes an exercise in curating roles and missions that resonate deeply with what young leaders believe to be their personal and professional callings.

In summary, adapting to the expectations of younger leaders calls for a seismic shift in traditional leadership models. A re-imagined approach that celebrates innovation, values diversity, actively engages in mentorship, leverages technology, and is grounded in social responsibility, flexibility, and authenticity will not only attract Gen Z talent but will also harness and amplify their unique strengths. As such, the companies that surmount these adaptive challenges will be well-placed to reap the benefits of a transformed, vibrant, and inclusive workplace, steered by leaders who are as dynamic as the times they exist in.

A focused adaptation by current leaders can catalyse the successful integration of Gen Z into the corporate world, transitioning from generational differences to collaborative strengths. It's through these concerted efforts that organisations will not just endure, but thrive, inspiring a new generation to redefine what leadership means in the modern age.

Traditional structures and norms are being re-evaluated and rewritten through the lens of a generation unencumbered by the 'way things have always been done'. Companies poised to lead in the years to come are recognising the imperative of not just welcoming Gen Z leaders, but of actively reshaping the corporate landscape in concert with their values and expectations. It's a bold step towards an uncertain yet undeniably exciting future.

Chapter 18:
Performance Management Revolutionised

As we pivot from the preparatory leadership frameworks discussed in Chapter 17, we're ushered into an era where performance management is not just reformed, but revolutionised, becoming a linchpin in harnessing the distinct potential of Generation Z. The traditional annual review is rapidly becoming an artefact of a bygone age, supplanted by dynamic, continuous feedback mechanisms that resonate with the immediacy Gen Z expects and thrives upon. Within this chapter, we delve into the intricacies of real-time analytics, where data isn't merely historic, but predictive and actionable. It's about curating a performance management ecosystem that is not only agile but also deeply integrated with the way Gen Z consumes information and interacts with the world. This is performance management reimagined; an interactive dance of feedback loops, analytics, and digital fluency that fosters not just growth, but a constant state of evolution, aligning with the generational ethos of perpetual progression and instantaneous innovation.

Continuous Performance Feedback Mechanisms

In an era where the speed of change matches Gen Z's appetite for instant gratification, traditional annual reviews are swiftly becoming relics of a bygone corporate culture. Instead, dynamic organisations are embracing continuous performance feedback mechanisms, a transformative move that not only aligns with younger generations' expectations but also enhances overall agility and responsiveness. At the heart of this shift lies a robust, open channel of communication that empowers employees with ongoing dialogues about their goals, achievements, and areas for improvement. This real-time feedback loop fosters a culture of growth and learning, integral for Generation Z who thirsts for frequent reassurance and opportunities to rapidly develop skills. Furthermore, it paves the way for a responsive and adaptive performance management system that keeps pace not only with organisational needs but also with the evolving professional landscape that Generation Z is stepping into.

Real-Time Analytics and Performance Tracking

Two concepts that carry immense weight in contemporary corporate settings, but even more so when applied to the integration of Gen Z into the workforce. A group that has grown up amidst the instantaneity of digital feedback, Gen Z employees not only expect but thrive on the same immediacy in the workplace. The ability to gauge performance in real-time and adjust actions accordingly is not just a fancy tool for this generation; it's an expectation, an intrinsic component of their work ethic.

The pursuit of real-time analytics reflects a move towards a culture that recognises the pace at which business operates today. We are witnessing a world where yesterday's achievements are rapidly overshadowed by the demands of the present. It's here that Gen Z's proclivity for quick feedback loops coincides with organisational needs for agile responsiveness. Implementing systems that provide real-time analytics allows leaders to monitor performance continuously, identify opportunities for instant feedback, and devise interventions that are relevant and immediate.

Furthermore, real-time analytics provide transparency that is highly valued by Gen Z workers. Their world is one where information is freely available; they understand the power it holds and expect openness within the workplace. By utilising analytics that provide insights into their performance, Gen Z is empowered to take control of their professional development, fostering a sense of autonomy and trust that is essential for their engagement.

Performance tracking, on the other hand, goes hand in hand with analytics but focuses on the longitudinal aspect of performance measurement. For Gen Z, the idea of annual reviews is as outdated as dial-up internet. They seek continuous appraisal and acknowledgment which performance tracking systems can provide. The utilisation of performance tracking tools can create a supportive environment where feedback is ongoing and professional growth is continuously encouraged.

As we adapt to the preferences of Gen Z, it becomes imperative to reassess traditional performance management systems. Gone are the days of top-down evaluations; feedback now flows in all directions. This two-way street, enhanced by technology, means that those at the helm must also be prepared to receive insights from their Gen Z counterparts. By embracing such fluid exchange, companies can stimulate an environment of collective improvement and shared accountability.

The emphasis on performance tracking shouldn't overshadow the importance of useability and user experience. Any system employed must be intuitive and engaging for this tech-savvy cohort. Overly complex or non-user-friendly platforms will serve as deterrents rather than motivators, potentially alienating Gen Z employees who value straightforwardness and efficiency.

Integrating real-time analytics into day-to-day operations also plays a crucial role in project management and client facing scenarios. In areas where Gen Z employees can see the direct impact of their contributions, their engagement and productivity levels often increase.

They appreciate seeing the fruits of their labour not yearly, not monthly, but in real-time.

But real-time analytics and performance tracking aren't solely about the immediate feedback for Gen Z. They enable predictive analytics, allowing leaders and employees alike to foresee potential challenges and address them proactively. For a generation that is focused on innovation and forward-thinking, this capability is not just a perk; it is an alignment of their personal aspirations with the futuristic orientation of their employers.

Moreover, performance tracking in the age of Big Data carries an added benefit for the organisation; it allows for more objective performance assessments. By relying on factual, data-driven insights, organisations can reduce biases that have historically plagued performance reviews. This approach promotes a meritocratic culture in which Gen Zers, who are highly sensitive to equity and fairness concerns, can fully buy-in.

Real-time analytics also contribute to a better understanding of collective and individual learning needs within an organization. As learning and development assume a more pivotal role in career progression, particularly for Gen Z, utilising analytics to tailor these initiatives will be increasingly important. The data-driven insights can aid in crafting personalised learning plans that cater to the strengths and areas for improvement of individuals, which is crucial for maintaining an engaged and competent Gen Z workforce.

The ethical dimensions of real-time analytics and performance tracking are also of paramount importance, given Gen Z's strong stance on privacy and data protection. Any systems implemented must uphold principles of transparency and user consent. Mismanagement of employee data could damage the trust and lead to disengagement from Gen Z, who are acutely aware of their digital footprint.

Adopting real-time analytics and performance tracking changes the role of HR and managers in engaging with employees. HR professionals, equipped with the latest tools and technologies, can now transition into roles that are as much about people analytics as they are about traditional HR functions. Similarly, managers must evolve into insightful coaches that utilise real-time feedback to guide and motivate their team members.

Impactful real-time analytics and performance tracking can only emerge from a culture that values data-driven decision-making while also recognising the human element at the core of its operations. These systems must not simply be about judging performance, but rather about fostering a work environment wherein continuous growth is part and parcel of the daily routine — a concept that resonates with the Gen Z ethos.

To conclude, the principles of real-time analytics and performance tracking are not new—sports teams, financial markets, and digital marketers have long relied on immediate data to tweak strategies and refine performances. However, their integration into workplace culture, especially for the benefit of Gen Z, represents the intersection of technological innovation with human capital management. For an organization to not just survive but flourish in the modern business landscape, embracing these tools is less an option and more a necessity, ensuring that every employee, particularly those from Gen Z, can advance in a workspace that values immediacy, fairness, and continuous improvement.

Chapter 19:
Marketing to Gen Z Consumers

In an era where traditional marketing strategies fall short, businesses must pivot their approach to resonate with Gen Z, a demographic that prizes authenticity, social responsibility, and digital fluency. As we delve into marketing to Gen Z consumers, it becomes crucial to understand the interplay between their consumer behaviour and their overarching life philosophies. Raised on a diet of rapidly changing social media platforms and global awareness, this generation demands transparency and alignment of brands with their personal values. This chapter unpacks the necessity of turning employees, particularly Gen Z ones, into brand advocates – a group whose endorsements are rooted in genuine brand experiences and can sway their peers in an authentic manner. Moreover, it's the age of storytelling, where a brand narrative is not merely conveyed but felt and experienced. Companies must craft compelling stories that speak to Gen Z's diverse, inclusive, and ethically-driven consciousness, ensuring customer engagement that doesn't just sell products but builds communities. These elements combined have the power to foster brand loyalty and drive consumer action among the most Internet-savvy generation to date. Engaging with Gen Z consumers therefore becomes more than a marketing strategy; it is a journey towards integrating organisational values with the expectations of tomorrow's leaders.

Turning Employees into Brand Advocates

As organisations strive to connect with the Gen Z consumer, turning employees into brand advocates emerges as a key strategy. The authenticity and relatability of Gen Zers espousing the virtues of their employer can resonate more effectively with their peers than traditional marketing approaches. To catalyse this transformation, companies must create environments that not only appeal to Gen Z values but also inspire loyalty and a genuine love for the brand.

Gen Z workers seek more than just a paycheck; they are drawn to organisations that align with their personal values and offer a sense of purpose in their roles. By tapping into these intrinsic motivators, employers can foster a workforce that is not only engaged but also eager to amplify the company's message.

Understanding Gen Z's penchant for transparency is crucial in this endeavour. This generation values open dialogue and a lack of pretence in business operations. They tend to endorse products and services they believe in vehemently, and conversely, are quick to voice dissent when their expectations of authenticity are unmet.

To harness the advocacy potential of Gen Z employees, companies must integrate the pursuit of social responsibility into their core missions. Initiatives aimed at community engagement, environmental sustainability, and ethical business practices can generate pride among workers. This pride, in turn, is shared across their social platforms, which are key battlegrounds for influencing consumer behaviour.

It's not just external branding efforts that benefit from Gen Z advocacy. An internal culture that celebrates diversity, fosters inclusion, and offers clear progression pathways can turn young employees into vocal champions for the organisation. When Gen Zers see their workplaces addressing issues like diversity, equality, and social justice, they're more likely to contribute their voices to the chorus singing their employer's praises.

Mentorship programs also play a pivotal role. Pairing Gen Z employees with seasoned professionals can enrich their work experience, making them feel valued and supported. These connections encourage Gen Zers to share their positive work experiences with their social circles, further extending the reach of the brand.

Developing a brand advocacy program can also be instrumental. By providing tools and incentives for employees to share their experiences and insights, organisations can empower their young workforce to become authentic spokespeople. Such programs can gamify the experience, offering rewards for those who actively promote the brand's message.

Furthermore, recognition plays a key part in this dynamic. Generously acknowledging contributions and achievements bolsters Gen Z workers' sense of ownership and commitment to the organisation. When they feel their input is genuinely valued, they're more likely to share their satisfaction and commitment with others.

Leadership styles must also evolve to accommodate this advocacy. Leaders who engage with their teams, openly share company successes and challenges, and draw on the collective intelligence of their workforce create a sense of camaraderie and unified mission.

However, authenticity must remain at the core of these efforts. Gen Z's adeptness in distinguishing between genuine advocacy and contrived marketing means traditional employee advocacy programs won't suffice. Instead, employers must cultivate genuine satisfaction and loyalty among their Gen Z workforce, encouraging them to naturally become brand advocates.

When it comes to articulating the vision and values of the company, organisations must ensure that Gen Z employees are well-versed. Inviting them to participate in town hall meetings, brainstorming sessions, and strategy discussions amplifies their understanding and thus, their ability to authentically endorse the company's objectives.

Given their digital savvy, providing Gen Z employees with social media guidance can amplify their advocacy efforts. Rather than imposing a stringent set of rules, offering training on effective online communication can help articulate the brand's narrative coherently while maintaining individual authenticity.

Another critical component is ensuring that the work environment, both physical and cultural, aligns with the aspirational lifestyle promoted by the brand. Gen Z employees will readily share their positive work experiences if they match the narratives touted by the employer's marketing message.

In conclusion, organically transforming employees into brand advocates relies on organisations embracing the ideals they convey to their consumers. By doing so, they leverage their Gen Z workforce's potential to connect with their peers and the broader consumer base. Ultimately, empowered Gen Z employees serve as the most valuable ambassadors an organisation can have in today's rapidly changing market.

The Power of Authenticity and Storytelling

As organisations grapple with the challenge of resonating with Generation Z consumers, the need for authenticity in marketing strategies has never been more pronounced. This digitally-savvy cohort, having grown up in a hyper-connected world, can discern genuine messages from contrived ones with uncanny accuracy. The art of storytelling, therefore, becomes a crucial tool in creating an authentic brand narrative that captivates and engages this young audience.

The narrative-driven campaigns that reverberate with Gen Z tap into their values and aspirations, encompassing a message that speaks to their collective experiences. Brands that acknowledge and celebrate the diversity in this generation's background, preferences, and perspectives will find a welcoming audience. Authenticity, coupled with storytelling that reflects Gen Z's lived realities, fosters a sense of trust and reliability.

Understanding the impact of a brand's story requires us to delve into the mechanisms of connection. Stories that narrate a journey, highlight struggles, and celebrate triumphs resonate with Gen Z's sense of progress and their desire for transparency. Through these narratives, brands are not merely purveyors of products but become entities with which consumers can establish an emotional bond, an aspect Gen Z deems indispensable.

Effective storytelling isn't merely about creating a narrative - it's about crafting experiences. With Technological immersion as second nature to Gen Z, their engagement with stories often materialises in interactive and immersive formats. Brands that harness Augmented Reality (AR) and Virtual Reality (VR) technologies to tell stories allow Gen Z to step into a world where they can relate to the brand's ethos in a tangible sense.

Yet, let's not conflate complexity with effectiveness. Sometimes, the most compelling tales are simple yet powerful, narrating everyday moments that encapsulate deeper meanings. A brand could foster a campaign that features real-life scenarios, user-generated content, or behind-the-scenes glimpses into its operations, thus appealing to Gen Z's preference for authenticity over polished perfection.

In the realm of social impact, cause-related storytelling can strongly appeal to Gen Z's social consciousness. Brands that align themselves with societal and environmental causes and articulate their commitment through stories exemplify the values that Generation Z cherishes. However, it is vital that these stories stem from genuine action rather than surface-level marketing.

Another significant dimension of using storytelling is the focus on co-creation. Encouraging Gen Z consumers to be part of the narrative by sharing their own stories and experiences creates a collaborative atmosphere. This transforms passive consumers into brand advocates, who in turn, infuse the brand's message with credibility and a multitude of unique perspectives.

When marketing to Gen Z, the authenticity in storytelling must also sustain itself across multiple channels to cater to their omnichannel presences, such as social media, blogs, and video platforms. Integrating and synchronising stories across these mediums ensures a cohesive brand message that Gen Z audiences can follow, no matter where they are.

Moreover, the role of influencers cannot be overstated in this equation. Gen Z is influenced by peer recommendations and the views of individuals they respect or aspire to be like. Partnerships with influencers who genuinely resonate with the brand's message can amplify authenticity and reach. The key lies in choosing partners who are authentic in their own right and whose stories align organically with the brand's values.

Responsiveness to real-time events and trends also elevates a brand's story in the eyes of Generation Z. They value brands with the agility to weave narratives that are culturally relevant and tuned into the zeitgeist. It demonstrates not only cultural awareness but also a brand's commitment to remaining a relevant and involved player in the lives of its consumers.

Importantly, when dealing with authenticity, any dissonance between what a brand says and what it does can lead to instant mistrust. Consistency between narrative and action provides a solid foundation for long-term relationships. Gen Z's connectivity allows them to instantly communicate discontent or praise, and they do not hesitate to hold brands accountable.

Crucially, storytelling is not a one-way street. The most influential brands listen as much as they broadcast, creating narratives that evolve with the feedback and input from Gen Z consumers. This iterative process ensures that stories remain true to brand values while reflecting the changing dynamics of the Gen Z audience.

The power of a brand lies not just in its ability to sell but in its ability to tell. A story that embraces authenticity and fosters a genuine connection can be the cornerstone of lasting brand loyalty among Gen Z consumers. As they ascend the economic ladder, their affinity for brands that live and breathe authenticity will likely determine the success stories of the future marketplace.

Therefore, companies aiming to market to Gen Z must invest time and resources in understanding this generation's core. They need to craft narratives that not only appeal to them but also involve them, respect them, and reflect them. In the landscape of the future, the brands that can embody and enact a tale of genuine engagement and shared values with Gen Z consumers are those that will stand apart.

In essence, for a generation that sifts through volumes of content daily, the brands that master the art of authentic storytelling are the ones that capture hearts. As we navigate the unique and complex sphere of marketing to Generation Z, we must remember that it's not just about what we sell; it's about the stories we tell and, more importantly, the realities that these stories create and represent.

Chapter 20:
Globalisation and Cultural Sensitivity

In a landscape where globalisation has erased many of the traditional barriers to cross-cultural engagement, the ability to work effectively with a diverse, international team is indispensable. Generation Z, with their inherent digital fluency and social connectivity, is at the vanguard of this global shift. This chapter delves into the intricate dance of cultural sensitivity where the workplace becomes an agile and vibrant tapestry of global perspectives. It's critical to understand that cultural intelligence is not merely an HR buzzword but a foundational element of modern business strategy. Companies that aspire to lead must inculcate a nuanced appreciation for diverse cultural norms and communication styles, tailoring approaches that resonate across continents. Embracing this diversity not only enriches the organizational culture but also widens the peerless problem-solving capabilities that diverse teams possess. This chapter guides strategic leaders in fostering an environment where Gen Z can maneuver through cross-cultural nuances with ease, ensuring that their multicultural workforce is not just present but fully engaged and contributing to the innovative thrust of a global enterprise.

Working Across Borders with Gen Z

In today's interconnected world, the notion of working across international borders has taken on new significance. For organisations aiming to harness the benefits of a globally diverse workforce, understanding Generation Z, the most freshly minted entrants into the job market, is not just advantageous but critical.

Generation Z's formative years were marked by rapid globalisation and digital connectedness. As a result, they bring a unique perspective to the workplace. They are digital natives, social media savants, and have grown up in a world where cross-cultural exchange is a daily occurrence. This blend of skills and experiences makes Gen Z employees an invaluable asset to businesses seeking to expand their global reach.

In leveraging the potential of Gen Z across borders, companies must first acknowledge the cultural nuances that shape the attitudes and expectations of these young professionals. Cultural intelligence is a must-have in the modern workplace, not just for dealing effectively with external clients and partners but also for tapping into the rich tapestry of insight that employees from diverse backgrounds provide.

Gen Z's global mindset extends to their working styles and preferences. Accustomed to seamless online interactions, they are well-suited for virtual teams that operate across different geographies. Including Gen Z in these global teams not only encourages innovation but also demonstrates a commitment to fostering an inclusive and multicultural work environment.

Effective Communication in a Cross-Border Context

Unsurprisingly, Gen Z communicates differently. Their day-to-day vocabulary is intertwined with the digital lingo and platforms they grew up using. Incorporating tools such as instant messaging apps and collaborative project management software makes it easier for them to integrate into and contribute to global work teams. But it's not just about the tools; it's about how they are used to facilitate transparent, authentic, and instant communication that respects diverse perspectives.

To thrive within these global contexts, businesses need to be cognizant of the communication barriers that might arise, both linguistic and cultural. Training programs can help Gen Z employees develop the intercultural communication skills they need to sidestep potential conflicts and misunderstandings. Additionally, fostering a company culture tolerant of mistakes allows for learning to happen through experience.

Gearing Up for Diverse Expectations in the Workplace

Gen Z's professional expectations are tied deeply to their personal values, which often include diversity and inclusivity, sustainability, and ethical transparency. As businesses pursue global agendas, aligning corporate practices with these values helps attract and retain Gen Z talent. They seek employers that don't just talk about making a difference but make it a reality—both locally and internationally.

It is not enough to create a veneer of inclusivity; businesses must integrate it into the core of their operations. This entails not only fostering a diverse workforce but also generating opportunities for Gen Z to engage with diverse markets, suppliers, and global issues directly related to their roles.

Remote Work, Mobility, and Gen Z

The modern workplace has seen a shift towards more flexible working arrangements. Gen Z workers, in particular, expect a level of mobility that allows them to work effectively from anywhere. This generation values jobs that offer the ability to balance their higher aspirations with personal commitments, and they believe this balance can be achieved remotely.

With increased remote work options, Gen Z can engage with international teams from their own homes, contributing to a business's global reach without the traditional costs and complexities of international relocation. Companies can harness this fluidity by offering mobility programs and remote work platforms that not only attract Gen Z talent but also help them work together across borders efficiently.

While the remote work paradigm brings flexibility, it is crucial to move beyond a one-size-fits-all approach. Sustainable remote work policies must consider different time zones, local cultural norms regarding work times, and the technological infrastructure available to Gen Z employees in different countries.

Mentorship and Collaborative Growth Across Borders

Mentorship is a powerful tool for the development of Gen Z professionals. Pairing them with seasoned colleagues from different cultural backgrounds can provide immense growth opportunities. It's through these mentorship partnerships that Gen Z can acquire nuanced understandings of cross-border interactions that they will not find in any textbook.

These types of collaborative experiences enrich the company as well, leading to a more culturally intelligent and sensitive workforce. Also, it is through hands-on collaboration that innovative solutions to complex global challenges are often born.

Finessing Global Talent Management

Adopting a global perspective in talent management is key to unlocking the potential of Gen Z. It's about creating systems of recognition, career development, and compensation that factor in and accommodate an international framework. Encouraging Gen Z to pursue international experiences and projects can also be a significant part of talent development.

Additionally, Gen Z's network-centric approach to professional relationships means they can be instrumental in expanding a company's international networks. Encouraging and enabling these connections positively impacts business development and talent attraction efforts.

Cultural Training and Competency

Global companies must put a premium on cultural competency training. Gen Z workers are primed to embark on learning journeys that enhance their ability to engage across cultures, but they require the tools and encouragement to do so effectively. This is where companies can step in to provide structured learning opportunities centred on cultural awareness and sensitivity.

This training must go beyond mere tolerance to cultivate a deep respect for cultural differences and a willingness to adapt business practices accordingly. It is through respect, understanding, and adaptation that businesses can truly meet the demands of today's complex international market.

Embracing Technological Innovations for Global Work

It is impossible to talk about working across borders with Gen Z without acknowledging their unique relationship with technology. For them, technological innovation is the benchmark of progress. They expect their employers to leverage contemporary tech to solve traditional problems.

Virtual Reality (VR), Augmented Reality (AR), and Artificial Intelligence (AI) can revolutionize the way global teams collaborate and interact. Utilizing these tools to facilitate 'virtual travel' and 'immersive meetings' can vastly enhance the global team experience for a demographic that values technological innovation.

In conclusion, Gen Z's natural predisposition towards digital fluency, a quest for inclusive cultures, and a desire to work with purpose aligns well with the multidimensional challenges and opportunities that globalisation presents to today's businesses. As companies aspire to a comprehensive understanding of this borderless landscape, integrating Gen Z into their global strategies can be the defining move towards a dynamic, inclusive, and innovative future.

Cultural Intelligence in the Modern Workplace

As the wave of globalisation sweeps across the world, the emphasis on cultural intelligence has burgeoned, becoming an indispensable asset within any forward-looking organisation. At the heart of this transformation lies a potent synergy between cultural sensitivity and a generational shift, courtesy of Generation Z, a cohort that prides itself on diversity and inclusiveness. Moreover, the flourishing global workplace demands a robust understanding of cultural intelligence, a term defining the capability to function effectively across diverse cultural contexts.

Companies striving for distinction in the marketplace recognise that to foster an environment where young, dynamic talent can thrive, cultural intelligence must be woven into the fabric of their corporate ethos. This integration speaks predominantly not just to the capacity for respect and understanding, but more critically to behavioural adaptation and the adoption of diverse perspectives in strategy, communication, and decision making.

Gen Z's arrival at the corporate threshold has heralded an era where seamless interaction across cultures is not just expected, it's mandatory. With their inherent global outlook, they bring a nuanced lens to cultural interpretation—an ability that when harnessed, augments organisational agility in the face of rapid global changes. Positioning cultural intelligence at the epicentre empowers teams to leverage the plethora of fresh insights and innovation that this younger generation holds.

Understanding and valuing the kaleidoscope of cultures that Gen Z represents requires a conscious effort to transcend traditional paradigms of workplace norms. Organizations must pivot from a monocultural mindset to a pluralistic approach, where cultural diversity is seen not as a challenge to overcome but as an opportunity to be embraced. This shift prompts a reevaluation of policies, practices, and privileges through a lens of equality and intersectionality.

Developing cultural intelligence is akin to crafting a tailored suit - it must fit the unique contours of each organisation. It starts with leadership that is not just aware but also empathetic to the plethora of cultural stimuli influencing their global workforce. The cultivation of this intelligence is a strategic advantage, enabling leaders to forge stronger connections within multigenerational and multicultural teams.

Training and development play a pivotal role in elevating cultural intelligence. Tailored programmes that focus on intercultural communication, conflict resolution, and collaborative problem-solving are key to equipping employees with the tools to thrive in a global setting. However, it isn't just about structured learning but also about fostering an environment where cultural learning is an experiential and continuous journey.

Recruitment strategies must align with the desire to build culturally intelligent teams. This means going beyond token diversity to seek a genuine representation that reflects the rich tapestry of the global talent pool. It's about finding individuals who not only excel in their respective roles but also demonstrate an acuity for cultural adaptability and an appreciation for global perspectives.

In the context of Gen Z, who have been digital natives since birth, technology serves as an enabler of cultural learning. Access to international collaborations, social networks, and a world of information online provides an unprecedented platform for cultural exchange and understanding. Organisations that leverage this affinity for technology can bridge cultural gaps more efficiently than ever before.

A culturally intelligent workplace is one where space is made for all voices to be heard. It's where collaborative technologies are used not just for project management or productivity but as platforms for the cross-pollination of ideas and fostering inclusive discussions where every cultural viewpoint is valued.

Mentoring isn't reserved only for skill development but is equally vital for cultural immersion. Pairing young employees with seasoned global veterans can create powerful mentorship dynamics that enable the organic transfer of cultural intelligence and global know-how.

Assessment and reflection are critical in ensuring that the path towards cultural intelligence doesn't veer off course. Regular check-ins, feedback mechanisms, and inclusive performance metrics ensure that the pursuit of cultural understanding is progressing and aligning with the overall organisational strategy.

The modern workplace also calls for policies that are not just diversity-focused but designed to empower employees to express their cultural identities confidently. This can manifest in flexible holidays that account for international observances, language assistance programmes, and creating spaces where cultural expression is not just accepted but celebrated.

Understanding the aspirations and motivations of Gen Z is integral to reaping the benefits of their cultural acumen. Their world view often includes a keen sense of global citizenship, and they are drawn to organisations that echo their values in social responsibility, equality, and global outreach.

It's also worth noting that cultural intelligence is a two-way street. While organisations must evolve to accommodate and nurture the cultural dynamism of Gen Z, these young workers in turn must be willing to engage with and respect the established cultures of their workplaces. This creates a balanced ecosystem where cultural synergies can thrive.

In conclusion, cultural intelligence in the modern workplace is not an optional extra but a strategic imperative. It is a key driver of innovation, cohesion, and agility in an increasingly complex global business environment. Organisations that master the nuances of this intelligence stand to become leaders in attracting and retaining the brightest minds of a generation poised to redefine the boundaries of what's possible in the workplace.

Chapter 21:
Sustainability As A Competitive Advantage

As we pivot from the comprehensive exploration of cultural intelligence and globalisation, Chapter 21 posits sustainability not merely as an ethical imperative, but an axis for strategic superiority in the evolving market. Gen Z's affinity for social responsibility coalesces with corporate lore that increasingly acknowledges the intrinsic value of sustainable practices. Companies that leverage environmentally-conscious operations don't just echo the sentiments of a demographic poised to populate the ranks; they carve a niche that distinguishes them in a competitive environment. These trailblazers gain not only the loyalty of a generation that champions green initiatives but also tap into systemic efficiencies that often translate to bottom-line benefits. The integration of eco-friendly practices becomes a synergy of brand enhancement, operational innovation, and fiscal prudence. By measuring the impact on people, planet, and profit, leaders can quantify sustainability's role as a cornerstone of contemporary business strategy, propelling their organizations to the forefront of a bold, conscientious, and profitable future.

Integrating Eco-Friendly Practices

Within the contemporary business landscape, sustainability isn't just a buzzword—it's a transformational ethos that distinguishes market leaders from their competition. Engaging eco-friendly practices not only appeals to the burgeoning consumer demand for ethical responsibility but also resonates deeply with Generation Z—a cohort which prioritises the planet's health as a critical component of employment decisions.

For organisations looking to leverage sustainability as a competitive advantage, the integration of eco-friendly practices must be genuine, strategic and interwoven with the company's core objectives. The process begins with a comprehensive understanding of what sustainability means within the context of each business. It's more than paper recycling initiatives or occasional 'green days'; it's about embedding eco-consciousness into every strand of the company's DNA.

An essential first step in this integration process is the audit of current practices. This scrutiny should cut across supply chains, energy consumption, resource utilisation and waste management. It's not merely an exercise in identifying shortcomings but a foundation for developing robust strategies that pave the way for incremental improvements that resonate with Gen Z's penchant for transparency and authenticity.

The next phase entails setting measurable targets. Sustainability must be quantified to gauge improvements accurately. Whether it's reducing carbon emissions, increasing the percentage of renewable energy used, or upping the recyclability of products, goals must be specific, and progress must be trackable. This approach sends a strong signal to Gen Z employees and consumers alike, that your business takes its environmental responsibilities seriously.

Communicating these ambitions and victories, no matter how small, becomes a narrative that defines the company's brand. Such discourse isn't a mere advertisement; it's a visceral display of commitment that Generation Z, equipped with their digital savviness and networking capabilities, can amplify across diverse platforms, further enhancing the organisation's standing in the sustainability conversation.

Collaborative efforts amplify impact. Partnerships with other businesses, non-profits, and governmental agencies can lead to innovative solutions that a single entity might not achieve. By pooling resources and knowledge, organisations can tackle significant environmental challenges and drive industry-wide changes, showcasing to Gen Z employees that they are part of a collective force for good.

Investment in technology and innovation is pivotal for furthering eco-friendly practices. From harnessing energy-efficient technologies to utilising data analytics for optimising resources, there's an array of innovative solutions capable of propelling environmental sustainability while also offering cost savings and operational efficiencies—a win-win for businesses and the environment.

Alongside technological investments, redesigning processes or even business models can manifest deeper green transformation. For instance, transition towards a circular economy that embodies reduced resource input, increased product life cycles, and the promotion of reuse and recycling can significantly mitigate environmental footprints and captivate the Gen Z workforce that is eager to witness and participate in meaningful change.

Developing a culture that fosters eco-consciousness at an individual level is vital. Eco-friendly practices resonate well when they become part of the daily routine and when staff members, especially from the Gen Z contingent, are empowered to bring forward their ideas on sustainability. Green incentives for employees can motivate adoption of eco-friendly behaviours, both inside and outside the office.

To truly engage with and uphold these practices, progressive appraisal and learning are necessitated. Continuous education on the significance of sustainability not only builds know-how but also keeps the momentum of eco-initiatives. Regular workshops, sustainability 'hackathons', and speaker events can kindle inspiration and innovation, driving the eco-agenda with vigour.

Eco-friendly practices should be embedded in the company's policies and the decision-making process. This calls for redefining procurement guidelines to favour sustainable suppliers, adjusting travel policies to reduce the carbon footprint, and integrating climate risks into business continuity planning. Such systemic changes exemplify a commitment that is tangible and influential beyond the confines of the company.

Engagement extends beyond internal operations to the consumer. A sustainable-minded organisation must educate and involve its customers in its green journey. Initiatives such as product take-back schemes or information provision on product sustainability scores help forge a connection with Gen Z consumers, who often make purchasing decisions based on the ethical positioning of a brand.

Feedback and progress tracking lie at the heart of sustainable practices. Regular monitoring and reporting keep all stakeholders informed and committed. It's crucial to not just document successes but also to candidly acknowledge areas where objectives fell short. This level of honesty is integral to the trust and respect of Gen Z, for whom integrity in environmental matters holds considerable weight.

Fostering innovation towards sustainability can also mean rethinking incentives and rewards. Building recognition programmes around achievements in sustainability encourages creativity and healthy competition. Employee engagement in green initiatives could even be tied to performance reviews, underscoring the significance placed on environmental stewardship.

Ultimately, integrating eco-friendly practices requires an astute approach that balances pragmatism with aspiration. As companies navigate through these uncharted territories, they emerge not only as stewards of the environment but as pioneers in the corporate world, carving spaces where Gen Z can exercise their values, environmental concerns, and innovative talents to shape a sustainable future for all.

Measuring Impact on People, Planet, and Profit

In the relentless pursuit of business success, a triadic consideration has forcefully surfaced, compelling companies to rethink their strategic imperatives. These are the impacts on people, planet, and profit—collectively known as the triple bottom line. This section explores how forward-thinking organizations, under the scrutinising eyes of Generation Z, measure their seismic imprint on these critical spheres. By quantifying discernible effects on human capital, the environment, and financial performance, businesses are not just responding to a moral calling, they're securing a competitive edge.

Firstly, let us delineate the 'people' aspect of this triad. Employees are not merely functionaries; they're the heart and sinew of any enterprise. Hence, the health, satisfaction, and development of staff constitute palpable metrics. Youthful cohorts, especially Gen Z, weigh the ethos of a workplace on the scales of diversity, equity, and meaningful engagement, prompting organizations to develop holistic approaches to measure and enhance employee wellbeing and empowerment.

When considering the planet, the environmental scorecard is ever-expanding. Businesses must scrutinize their carbon footprint, waste reduction efforts, and resource utilisation. Sustainability reports are becoming more than voluntary disclosures; they are tools of accountability and transparency. Gen Z's eco-consciousness necessitates that corporations not just pay lip service to environmental stewardship but confirm their commitment through verified reductions in greenhouse gas emissions and sustainable sourcing practices.

Turning to profit, traditional financial metrics such as revenue growth and net income remain pivotal. However, there's now a burgeoning recognition that long-term profitability is inextricably linked to social and environmental performance. Companies investing in renewable energy, for instance, can often foresee future cost savings. Similarly, organizations that foster strong community relations can cultivate consumer loyalty, translating into sustained revenue streams.

To appraise people impact, one must venture beyond perfunctory employee satisfaction surveys. Forward-thinking firms are incorporating a suite of qualitative and quantitative indicators, from turnover rates to sentiment analysis derived from internal communication channels. Moreover, the ascension of workplace analytics enables a deeper understanding of collaboration patterns, productivity inhibitors, and drivers of employee engagement.

Environmental impact measurement is both intricate and imperative. It bridges the gap between intention and actuality, and it harnesses the power of data—be it in tracking energy consumption or assessing supply chain sustainability. Leading organizations are deploying digital tools to capture real-time environmental data, facilitating responsive and informed decision-making. For Gen Z, the voracity of environmental claims is often a deciding factor in both their consumption and employment choices.

When it ties back to profit, metrics stretch across a broad spectrum. Socially responsible investments can be gauged for their returns, just as customer and employee retention can be correlated with ethical practices. The foresighted enterprise decodes patterns within these metrics to navigate the market with agility, all while demonstrating a genuine commitment to social and environmental codes which resonate deeply with Gen Z values.

Metrics like Net Promoter Score (NPS) are evolving to incorporate social and environmental factors, providing a more holistic understanding of brand reputation and loyalty. Furthermore, Integrated Reporting is gaining traction, combining financial with non-financial data to give stakeholders a comprehensive view of an organisation's sustainable performance.

To assuage the scepticism that often greets corporate sustainability assertions, third-party certifications and audits have ascended in prominence. The likes of B Corp or ISO 14001 offer a stamp of credibility to an organization's endeavours, ensuring that measures taken are not just for show but are leading to verifiable enhancements in sustainability performance.

Community engagement and the corresponding social impact are also scrutinized through the prism of generational expectations. Gen Z's insistence on societal contribution necessitates that businesses quantify their outreach and societal investments. Whether it's by calculating volunteer hours, tracking philanthropic expenditures, or measuring the socio-economic impacts of community programs, corporations can no longer bask in vague proclamations of 'giving back'.

Alignment with the United Nations Sustainable Development Goals (SDGs) provides a robust framework for aligning business objectives with global priorities. Adopting these goals can help streamline an organization's focus and provides a universally recognized language for reporting sustainability achievements and challenges.

In the realm of human impact, the proliferation of wellbeing initiatives reflects a shift towards comprehensive employee care. Progressive businesses are examining how workplace designs support mental health, how policies foster inclusivity, and how learning and growth opportunities align with personal aspirations. For Gen Z, who prioritize mental health and personal fulfillment, these are decisive factors in choosing an employer.

Data algorithm sophistication now underpins increasingly accurate predictive analytics. Evaluating environmental risks and their potential economic consequences enables businesses to preemptively address vulnerabilities. These analytics also aid in measuring the cost-effectiveness of sustainability initiatives over the long term.

Ultimately, a focus on the people, planet, and profit metrics clarifies an organization's purpose and strategy. It's about capturing and communicating the full array of impacts arising from business activities. By presenting cogent and quantifiable sustainable narratives, companies forge trust amongst a generation that demands factual substantiation. Gen Z isn't just passing through—they're redefining the pathways of success for those brands perceptive enough to see the longevity in sustainable excellence.

In conclusion, as businesses recalibrate their compass to navigate the Gen Z-initiated currents of change, they're discovering that sustainability isn't a peripheral activity; it's central to their future trajectory. By meticulously measuring impact on people, planet, and profit, they don't just excel in moral spheres; they rehearse the future language of business, one that speaks with conviction about value creation in its most comprehensive form.

Chapter 22:
The Future of Work and Gen Z

In delving into Chapter 22, we must turn our gaze firmly towards the horizon where the future of work intersects with the aspirations and ingenuity of Generation Z. This cohort, having honed a unique set of digital skills and a distinctive outlook on employment, is now prompting a radical reimagining of the workplace—where flexibility, autonomy, and purpose are not mere perks, but essential ingredients of a fulfilling career path. The workplaces that will thrive in the coming years are those that recognize and harness Gen Z's potent blend of tech-savviness and their quest for impactful work. As such, organisations are tasked with creating ecosystems brimming with innovation, underscored by a strong ethical compass, and above all, agile in the face of ever-shifting employment paradigms. For leadership, this signifies a departure from convention, an embrace of fluid structures, and an unwavering commitment to nurturing spaces where Gen Z's vibrant potential can be fully realized, setting the stage for a dynamic symbiosis between the workers of tomorrow and the forward-thinking entities that will undoubtedly prosper from their fresh perspectives and prodigious talents.

Predicting Workplace Trends

As the contemporary workplace merges inexorably with the future, discerning trends that resonate with Generation Z is no mere speculative exercise but a strategic imperative. With their fingertip feel for technological integration, Gen Z's rise heralds a profound shift towards an economy that prizes flexibility, autonomy, and purpose with unprecedented fervour. Prognostications suggest a surge in career paths that eschew the traditional linear trajectory, leaning instead into a matrix of experiences enriched by a digital thread. Tomorrow's organisations must weave adaptability into their DNA to accommodate the quicksilver pace of change and talent fluidity that Generation Z both drives and desires. Furthermore, we're witnessing an emergent emphasis on work models that harmonise with individual values and societal impact—here, purpose isn't simply a buzzword but a fundamental principle shaping Gen Z's vocational choices. As we peer into this evolving landscape, those who can anticipate and act upon these inclinations will be the architects of a resolutely human-centric and innovative workplace—a beacon for the upcoming wave of digital-native professionals.

Flexibility, Autonomy, and Purpose-Driven Careers

The insatiable demand for flexible work arrangements is a cornerstone of the Gen Z ethos, fundamentally challenging the traditional 9-to-5 work paradigm that has dominated for decades. This generation has come of age during a time of quantum leaps in technology and continuous socio-economic shifts, spawning a preference for work-life integration rather than the ill-fitting pursuit of balance. They don't just see work as a place to go, but as a task to be completed – whether from home, a café, or across continents.

Organisations must now pivot to provide this flexibility as standard, embedding it into the DNA of corporate culture. By embracing remote work technologies and developing robust policies for asynchronous work, businesses can attract Gen Z talent who are adept at managing their time and deliverables without constant supervision. But it's not just about the where and when of work; it's also about the how. Gen Zers relish the opportunity to shape their own workflows and innovate on the job, making autonomy not just a perk but a necessity for their professional satisfaction.

The impetus for a purpose-driven career is another clarion call from Gen Z. Long gone are the days when mere monetary compensation could secure loyalty and enthusiasm. Gen Z seeks a deeper connection to their work, a sense of contributing to something larger than themselves. They hunger for missions and ideals that resonate with their personal values, for companies that don't just pay lip service to global issues but take tangible action on social justice, environmental sustainability, and community upliftment.

To retain this cohort, businesses need to articulate and demonstrate a clear ethos that aligns with Gen Z values. Companies should not be afraid to take a stand on social issues or to weave their corporate social responsibility programmes into the fabric of their daily operations. Engaging Gen Zs in these initiatives, giving them agency to lead projects or decide where company efforts should be focused, only strengthens their commitment and investment in their roles.

Gen Z's preference for flexibility and autonomy also translates into how they view career progression. The standard ladder climbing of yesteryears does not entice them; instead, they prefer a career lattice where they can move laterally, explore different roles, and develop a portfolio of experiences and skills. Skills development and continuous learning are critically important to them, and they often seek roles that offer the promise of growth personally and professionally.

Leaders must adapt development programmes and career models to accommodate this non-linear approach to career advancement. Offering rotations, shadowing opportunities, and cross-departmental projects can satisfy this demographic's thirst for variety and challenge in their career journey. This approach not only nurtures their multifaceted skillset but can also foster interdisciplinary innovation within the organisation.

Professional autonomy to Gen Z also means entrepreneurial freedom. They have grown up with the tools to create and monetise their passions at their fingertips and often have side projects that they value highly. Companies that recognise and support these pursuits – within reason and without conflicts of interest – can engender loyalty and potentially harness these side ventures for mutual gain. It's a matter of respecting the multi-dimensional nature of the Gen Z workforce.

When it comes to performance management, traditional annual reviews feel antiquated to this fast-paced, feedback-hungry generation. They crave continuous dialogue and real-time feedback that allows them to adjust and improve promptly. Performance tracking systems need to evolve towards more frequent and informal check-ins that align with the dynamic pace at which Gen Z operates.

Understanding and integrating Gen Z's need for flexibility, autonomy, and purpose in their careers is not just an HR issue – it's strategic business sense. An enlightened leadership perspective recognises that when employees, particularly those entering the workforce, are engaged on these levels, they bring innovation, commitment, and a forward-thinking approach that can propel the entire organisation forward.

Today's executives need to adopt a multifaceted view that values the individual as a whole, understanding that Gen Zers cannot leave their idiosyncrasies at the door. Instead, they bring their full selves to work, expectations and all. Inclusion of diverse perspectives, sensitivity to personal well-being, and attention to ethical practices align to make the Gen Z workforce a formidable force of change and progress.

Encouraging flexibility and autonomy while fostering a strong sense of purpose within careers will not only satisfy Gen Z but will also revitalise the entire workforce. This alignment between personal and organisational values allows employees at all levels to feel more connected to their work, leading to higher levels of engagement and performance.

Firms that reconfigure their practices in line with these principles will be on the leading edge. They'll be the ones who not only attract and keep the best Gen Z talent but also set the stage for a culture of innovation, inclusivity, and sustainability. Far from being a concession, adapting to Gen Z's workstyle preferences is a competitive advantage, a means of future-proofing a business in a rapidly evolving commercial landscape.

As we look towards the chapters ahead, it's evident that engaging Gen Z employees, nurturing entrepreneurial traits, and preparing leaders for this new workforce are all interconnected facets that build on Gen Z's foundational needs for flexibility, autonomy, and purpose. With the appropriate strategies, organisations can harness the unique strengths of Gen Z to drive business success and create a dynamic and resilient future.

Chapter 23:
Overcoming Resistance to Change

As we pivot from discovering how to leverage flexibility, autonomy, and purpose in crafting careers that resonate with Generation Z, we are confronted with the immutable challenge of overcoming resistance to change within the organisational fabric. This evolution requires a persuasive approach, which is met with an assortment of psychological barriers that hold the potential to stagnate progress. To navigate through these turbulent waters, change agents must employ expository tactics that lend themselves to methodical persuasion, underscoring the rationale and benefits of the transformative roadmap ahead. With a journalistic lens, we must probe the undercurrents of trepidation that accompany shifts in organisational culture and practices. Building resilience—both at the grassroots and executive levels—is critical in ensuring a company's enduring agility. By layering the understanding of Gen Z's aspirations with strategic change management, executives can erect a bridge across the chasm of resistance, crafting an environment wherein innovation and inclusivity aren't merely aspired to, but embodied.

Methods for Smooth Transitions

In the ever-evolving business landscape, it's imperative that companies adapt to welcome the fresh perspectives and digital fluency of Generation Z. Introducing change can often be met with resistance from existing workforce layers. As such, smooth transition methods are crucial for successful and harmonious integration without compromising productivity.

One such method is a well-defined communication strategy. It's essential to articulate the rationale for change, detailing how it aligns with the organisation's vision and the mutual benefits to all employees. Transparent and ongoing communication alleviates uncertainty and builds trust, serving as a strong foundation for the forthcoming modifications.

Another key approach revolves around gradual implementation. Sudden changes can evoke anxiety and push-back. Instead, staging the introduction of new processes allows employees of various generational cohorts to digest and acclimatise to new ways of working, especially when these processes are technology-driven—a realm where Generation Z shines.

Engaging Gen Z as peer mentors can also facilitate smoother transitions. Utilising their technological know-how and fresh perspectives can assist other employees in navigating new digital tools and working styles, fostering a culture of collaboration and continuous learning.

Inclusion in decision-making processes can also significantly mitigate resistance. When employees are involved in the planning and execution stages of transition, they're more likely to feel invested in the change and become willing participants rather than reluctant bystanders.

Change champions and influencers within the organisation can be instrumental during transitions. Identifying and empowering key personnel who are respected by their peers to advocate for the change can create a positive narrative around the transition, influencing others to follow suit.

Training and upskilling are fundamental in ensuring smooth transitions. Providing adequate training for new technologies, processes, or roles helps build competence and confidence among the workforce, effectively reducing the fear of the unknown that often accompanies change.

Implementing pilot programs before a full-scale rollout is an effective way of identifying potential issues and gathering feedback. It allows for a testing phase where tweaks can be made before every employee is affected, thus demonstrating a commitment to getting it right for everyone's benefit.

Leadership plays a critical role in any transition. Leaders must not only "talk the talk" but "walk the walk." By leading by example and showing enthusiasm for the new direction, leaders can inspire their teams and guide them through change with a demonstrated commitment.

Celebrating small wins along the road to full implementation injects positivity into the transition process. Acknowledging milestones and improvements, no matter how minor, can boost morale and underscore the progress being made thanks to everyone's efforts.

Feedback mechanisms should be put in place to hear the voice of the workforce throughout the transition. Regular check-ins, surveys, and suggestion boxes allow employees to express concerns and contribute ideas, ensuring that everyone feels heard and valued.

Attention must also be paid to workloads during transition phases. Overburdening employees with change on top of their day-to-day tasks can lead to burnout and resistance. Appropriate pacing and support during transitions are essential in maintaining staff well-being.

Understanding the diverse reactions to change is also important. Personalising support and offering varied resources—like one-on-one coaching, team workshops, or self-paced online modules—can cater to the various ways in which employees adapt to change.

Maintaining consistency in the face of change is paradoxical yet necessary. Upholding the core values and mission of the organisation, even as new methods are adopted, provides a stable backdrop against which change occurs, making transitions less jarring.

Lastly, offering reassurance on job security can alleviate one of the primary concerns tied to organisational change. Addressing this directly and reassuring employees that the intention of integrating Gen Z innovations is to enhance, rather than replace, the current workforce can quell many fears and resistances.

By considering these methods for smooth transitions, organisations can significantly reduce the barriers to integrating Generation Z into the workforce. The ultimate goal is to create an environment that celebrates diversity in thought and experience, leveraging the unique skills of every generation to drive innovation and secure a prosperous future.

Building Resilience in Organisations and Individuals

In navigating the waters of organisational change, resilience emerges as the keystone of success. As we had previously explored methods for smooth transitions in the face of resistance, it's imperative to delve into the core attributes that underpin resilience both at an individual and organisational level. Building resilience is not simply about weathering the storm, but thriving amidst the ongoing challenges that the integration of Generation Z into the workforce presents.

Organisational resilience is a multi-dimensional construct that aligns with the capacity to adapt to new situations while maintaining core functions. It's the agility to change course when necessary and the foresight to anticipate shifts in the market or workforce. In this light, cultivating resilience within an organisation necessitates an understanding of both structural and cultural facets that underpin adaptability.

Nurturing a resilient culture within an organisation translates into fostering an environment where individuals are empowered to embrace change rather than fear it. This involves promoting a culture of continuous learning and personal development, which is particularly resonant with Gen Z employees, who value growth and progression. By investing in training and creating avenues for skills development, organisations can encourage a workforce that is ready to tackle the challenges of tomorrow.

It's important to acknowledge the interplay between individual and organisational resilience. Individuals shape organisational culture and organisational practices, in turn, influence individual behaviours. Therefore, supporting the personal resilience of employees is crucial. This can be achieved through initiatives that focus on mental health and well-being, such as mindfulness programs or flexible working arrangements that allow employees to manage their work-life balance more effectively.

Communication lies at the heart of resilience-building efforts. Clear and transparent communication regarding upcoming changes demystifies the process, mitigates uncertainty, and fosters a sense of stability even in times of flux. Utilising channels that resonate with a tech-savvy generation, like social media and collaborative platforms, ensures messages are not only disseminated but also welcomed and engaged with by your Gen Z cohort.

Resilient organisations also possess an inherent capacity for innovation. Embracing a mindset that's aligned with Gen Z's entrepreneurial spirit serves to catalyse new approaches to problem-solving and steers the company away from stagnation. Creating a safe space for innovation, where risks are managed and even failure is seen as a stepping stone to success, nurtures a culture that responds dynamically to change.

Diversity and inclusivity are key aspects of resilience, and organisations must be proactive in weaving these elements into the very fabric of their culture. Encouraging varying perspectives leads to richer problem-solving and a more agile response to changing market and workforce dynamics. Inclusivity here is not just a buzzword but a strategic imperative that leverages a plethora of experiences, backgrounds, and insights in stewarding resilience.

To ensure these concepts are not just theoretical, embedding resilience training into leadership development programs is crucial. Leaders set the tone for an organisation's response to change, and thus, equipping them with the tools to be resilient decision-makers and compassionate guides is essential. Such training should include aspects of emotional intelligence, crisis management, and strategic foresight.

Furthermore, the resilience of an organisation can often be traced back to its foundational values. A value-driven company, where decisions and actions are aligned with a shared set of principles, offers employees a consistent and reliable framework which in times of change, acts as a stabilising force. The alignment with Gen Z's desire for purpose-driven careers cements a company's resilience through a unified sense of direction.

Resilience can also be fostered by engaging in scenario planning and stress testing. By preparing for a variety of potential futures, organisations can identify potential threats and opportunities early on. This proactive stance embraces change as an inevitable aspect of the business landscape, preparing both individuals and organisations to pivot when needed.

The role of HR in building resilience cannot be overstated. HR strategies must be designed to identify and address the human factors that contribute to an organisation's resilience. From recruitment to retirement, ensuring that resilience is consistently reinforced through policies, practices, and the overall employment experience is fundamental.

Financial resilience is another significant aspect, especially when integrating a new generation into the workforce. An understanding of Gen Z's financial expectations and aspirations is vital in developing compensation models that are both sustainable for the organisation and satisfactory for the employees. Aligning financial strategies with broader organisational resilience ensures a solid base from which to evolve.

Technological resilience, especially in an era dominated by digital natives, cannot be overlooked. With Gen Z workers expecting cutting-edge tools and platforms for their professional endeavours, ensuring that your company's technology can withstand and evolve with the rapid pace of change is paramount. This means not only investing in the latest tech but also maintaining robust cybersecurity measures to protect against potential online threats.

Lastly, measuring and tracking the development of resilience within an organisation provides tangible feedback on progress and identifies areas for improvement. Adopting real-time analytics and other performance tracking tools allows for a transparent understanding of where the organisation stands and where it needs to bolster its efforts.

In conclusion, building resilience is a complex, yet critical, endeavour in the modern business environment. It involves a symphony of strategic planning, cultural alignment, and individual empowerment. As we prepare to welcome Generation Z into our ranks, embedding resilience into the DNA of our organisations will pave the way for a future that not only endures but thrives in the face of relentless change.

Chapter 24:
Success Stories and Case Studies

As we pivot from understanding the theoretical aspects of integrating Generation Z into the workplace to the tangible, the narrative of success stories and case studies becomes paramount. This chapter delves into a collection of companies that have not only embraced the inclusion of Gen Z but have also reaped the rewards of a rejuvenated, future-ready workforce. It examines the practical applications and best practices implemented within notable organisations, delineating the roadmap from strategic vision to actionable outcomes. Whether it's a tech startup that's mastered the art of agile innovation with its young talent or a legacy enterprise that's undergone a radical transformation to resonate with Gen Z values, these case studies showcase the diverse approaches and transformative impacts of aligning with the aspirations and ethos of the youngest tier of employees. By dissecting the successes, we imbue our own strategies with evidence-based confidence, underscoring the potential for dynamism that Gen Z infuses into an organisation's DNA when effectively integrated.

Practical Applications and Best Practices

In drawing lessons from successful integrations of Generation Z into the workforce, it's imperative to pinpoint practical applications and best practices that have emerged from these transitions. Companies making strides in this regard often foster environments where adaptive leadership, flat organisational structures, and digital fluency aren't just buzzwords, but lived experiences for their teams. They champion innovative recruitment strategies to attract Gen Z talent—pioneering techniques that resonate with the values and communication styles of this cohort. By tailoring onboarding processes and professional development programmes, such companies confirm that an agile approach can enhance learning outcomes and fit the lifestyle of these digital natives. Furthermore, best practices include actionable insights on blending technology with humanity, ensuring that Gen Z's concern for sustainability and social responsibility is woven into the company culture. It's through the stories of these thriving organisations that leaders can distil the essence of what makes a workplace truly Gen Z-centric—and in turn, position their own enterprises at the forefront of future-focused innovation and growth.

Companies That Have Successfully Integrated Gen Z

Turning our attention to real-world applications, it becomes clear that many forward-thinking companies have made remarkable strides in integrating Generation Z into their operations. They have not only attracted young talent but have successfully harnessed their unique competencies and viewpoints to achieve innovative outcomes and bolster the workplace dynamic.

Take, for example, a tech giant that reimagined its internship programs to attract Gen Z talent. Recognising the value of early-career insights into technology and consumer trends, it revamped traditional hierarchies. Interns are given significant projects and a voice in meetings, aligning with Gen Z's desire for meaningful work and impact.

Another success story comes from a multinational consumer goods company that puts sustainability at the core of its business strategy. This resonates deeply with Gen Z's passion for environmental issues, making the brand an employer of choice. Initiatives like sustainability hackathons and eco-friendly product lines are direct results of Gen Z's influence.

Financial service firms have also had to adapt to the digital proficiency of Gen Z. One such company launched a digital-first banking platform catering to the preferences of younger generations for online transactions and financial management—all designed with Gen Z input, from user interface to security features.

Fashion and retail sectors aren't far behind; one apparel brand has gained traction among Gen Z by integrating social media influencers into its design and marketing processes, recognising the platforms where Gen Z spend significant time and exert considerable influence.

Additionally, several companies across various industries have seen fruitful results from investing in mentorship programs. These programs offer Gen Z workers access to industry experts, embodying a commitment to collaborative growth and development that Gen Z prizes highly.

One multinational corporation stands out for altering its workspace design. In an effort to nurture Gen Z's preference for collaboration and versatility, the company introduced flexible workspaces that can be modified to suit the task at hand, whether it be collaborative projects or individual focus work.

Furthermore, some organisations have been pioneers in offering remote work options, tapping into Gen Z's seek for balance and autonomy. These companies have employed advanced digital collaboration tools to ensure that even remote work is engaging and inclusive.

Another tech company has made waves with its in-house microlearning platform. Recognising Gen Z's penchant for quicker, more digestible learning experiences, they've managed to increase engagement and enhance skill acquisition.

A leading consultancy firm redefined its performance management system to provide continuous feedback, in sync with Gen Z's desire for regular and constructive communication regarding their work and career progression.

Healthcare is another sector where Gen Z's influence is evident. A prominent healthcare provider has introduced mental health days and encourages open conversations about wellbeing in the workplace, which aligns perfectly with Gen Z's concerns about mental health and wellbeing.

The hospitality industry is also adapting, with one hotel chain integrating local culture into its properties, thereby appealing to Gen Z's appreciation for authenticity and immersive experiences. Employees are encouraged to bring forward local initiatives and community engagement projects.

A standout case in the legal sector involves a law firm creating digital hubs that not only cater to Gen Z's digital-first approach but also foster an environment for these young professionals to contribute to the firm's innovation in legal tech.

In the manufacturing sector, a company has not just mechanised its processes but has also invited Gen Z to lead the charge in implementing AI and machine learning solutions to optimise production and minimise environmental impact.

Last but certainly not least, several organisations are revising compensation models to include non-traditional benefits like student loan assistance, aligning with Gen Z's financial goals and their acute awareness of economic challenges.

These exemplary cases show a willingness to evolve, to listen, and to integrate the perspectives of Generation Z into the fabric of organisational life. The companies that have done this successfully are a testament to the innovation and growth that comes from embracing the strengths of this dynamic generation and setting a benchmark for others to follow.

Chapter 25:
Preparing For The Alpha Generation

In anchoring the values and practices discussed so far, we're not merely pitching our tent with Generation Z. We must pivot our gaze further to the horizon and start laying the groundwork for the arrival of the Alpha Generation—the cohorts born from 2010 onwards. As futurist-minded leaders, we're tasked with an invigorating challenge: envisioning and molding a workplace pliable enough to accommodate the technologically engrossed, yet-to-be-defined workforce of tomorrow. It's a place where continuous adaptation and a culture of lifelong learning aren't just encouraged but are intrinsic to the organisational DNA. Gen Alpha will step into a professional world rich with AI, virtual ecosystems, and quantum leaps in communication, thus expecting a symphony of innovation and flexibility that we must begin composing today. As we shepherd in this new age, it's critical that we engrain the lessons learnt with Gen Z, while boldly embracing the exponential changes that lie ahead—fostering an environment that resonates with the core of what it means to be digitally native, cognitively agile, and boundlessly creative.

Looking Beyond Gen Z

As we consider the impact and integration of Generation Z into the workforce, it's imperative to also cast our eyes further afield—to the Alpha Generation. Those born from approximately 2010 onwards may seem distant figures on the workforce horizon, but they are the future employees, consumers, and leaders who will continue the transformative trends started by their predecessors. This section delves into the anticipated characteristics of this nascent generation and how forward-thinking organisations can begin to prepare for their eventual integration into the business landscape.

The Alpha Generation is poised to grow up in a hyper-connected world where technology is an even more seamless part of daily life. Unlike Gen Z, who saw the rise of digital technology, Alphas are born into it; they are expected to interact with technology in an intuitive and integrated manner that surpasses the proficiency of those before them. For businesses, this means an impending need to revamp technological infrastructure to be even more innovative, intuitive, and intrinsic to daily operations.

The trend towards remote and flexible working arrangements, strongly favoured by Gen Z, will likely escalate with Generation Alpha. The concept of a traditional office may seem archaic to Alphas, who could view the flexibility of location and schedule not just as a perk, but as a fundamental expectation. Organizations need to ensure their operational and performance management frameworks are adaptable to cater to a highly mobile and autonomous workforce.

Gen Z's values around sustainability, inclusivity, and corporate responsibility are likely to become even more pronounced with Alpha. Since they will mature in an age where these issues are at the forefront of public discourse, Alpha's career choices may gravitate towards organizations that demonstrate a genuine commitment to making a positive societal impact. It will become crucial for businesses to embed these values into their core to attract and retain Alpha talent.

The learning and development platforms of today must evolve to cater to Alpha's learning preferences, which are likely to include advanced gamification and immersive experiences through virtual and augmented reality. As continuous learners, Alphas will expect education to be a mix of digital and experiential learning, both highly personalized and on-demand. Organizations will need to consider these preferences to design effective upskilling programs.

Communication styles within the workplace will need further evolution to match Alpha's mode of interaction. With Gen Z already displaying a preference for visual and video content, Alpha will likely take this further, potentially reinventing the norms of professional communication. Companies need to foresee these changes and equip their teams with the right tools and platforms to facilitate this new dialog.

Organizational structures will need to continue evolving. Given the trajectory set by Gen Z's collaborative and flexible work approach, Alpha may take it to new heights, potentially dissolving traditional hierarchies even further to favour fluid, project-based teams and roles. Executives must be able to lead within these dynamic structures while still maintaining a clear strategic direction and performance measures.

Product and service design will be affected as well, with Alphas likely looking for unparalleled levels of customization and instantaneity. Their consumer behaviour could redefine loyalty and brand engagement, pushing companies to be ever more innovative and responsive to individual preferences. The implications for marketing and product development teams are vast and will require a strategic foresight to navigate effectively.

Data privacy will become even more critical as Generation Alpha's data footprint expands. The concerns Gen Z has about privacy and data security will be intensified in this future cohort, compelling companies to be transparent and secure about their data handling practices to an unprecedented degree. Trusted relationships will be built on the responsible use of data.

The entrepreneurial drive seen in Gen Z is likely to be amplified within Alpha, with many having access to unprecedented technological resources and platforms to innovate from an early age. Businesses will benefit from harnessing this entrepreneurial energy early, encouraging innovation and potentially partnering with Alpha entrepreneurs to co-create groundbreaking solutions.

As workplace automation and AI continue to advance, the Alpha Generation may experience the abolishment of certain traditional career paths, creating a landscape where adaptability and creativity are paramount. Companies should focus on fostering a culture of innovation that can anticipate and respond to the resulting changes in workforce dynamics and job scopes.

The potential engagement of Alphas with the emerging gig economy could influence a new paradigm in job security and employee benefits. Organizations may need to redefine what professional stability means and how they offer support to a workforce that values flexibility over permanency.

In the context of globalization, Alphas are likely to have an even greater global mindset than Gen Z. They will naturally expect to work in diverse environments that are fully integrated across borders, demanding organizational cultural intelligence and global collaboration capabilities. This international perspective will be crucial both for teams and the leaders who guide them.

While much of Generation Alpha's characteristics are projections, these individuals are already influencing market trends and family purchasing decisions. Their digital fluency, dynamic learning style, values-led ethos, and native globalism are clear markers that demand attention. HR strategies, workplace environments, and business models will have to evolve to meet the needs and leverage the potential of this rising generation.

In preparing for the entrance of Generation Alpha, the most crucial mindset for executors and strategists is to acknowledge that they're not planning for a fixed point in the future but for a constantly shifting landscape. An environment of continuous adaptation and lifelong learning, a theme that will be further explored, is key to ensuring that organizations not only remain relevant but thrive in the decades to come.

Continuous Adaptation and Lifelong Learning

The landscape of work is ever-evolving, with successive generations introducing new perspectives and prompting shifts in the workplace environment. As we prepare for the emergence of the Alpha Generation, it is paramount that we don't just focus on the immediate horizon, but also foster a culture that prizes continuous adaptation and lifelong learning.

Historically, most professionals could expect to acquire a set of skills early in their careers that would serve them well for decades. This model is no longer viable in the fast-paced, ever-changing business world where the Alpha Generation will operate. Fostering a mindset of lifelong learning is critical; it's the bedrock upon which future-ready employees can continuously evolve their capabilities in alignment with emerging technologies and shifting industry demands.

So, what does this mean for organizations as they integrate not only Gen Z but also look ahead to the Alpha Generation? It requires a fundamental shift in how learning and development are structured within the corporate ecosystem. Traditional, structured training methods may give way to more dynamic, on-demand, and personalised learning experiences engineered to adapt to individual needs and professional growth trajectories.

These learning experiences aren't just about building hard skills but are equally focused on cultivating soft skills, such as adaptability, critical thinking, and emotional intelligence, that are paramount in a world where automation and AI are increasingly prevalent. Empowering employees to hone these skills will prepare them to navigate uncertain territories, innovate in face of challenges, and collaborate effectively with diverse teams.

Moreover, as the Alpha Generation steps into the workplace, they will not only be digital natives but may also be known as 'learning natives', expecting and anticipating opportunities for growth as part of their career journey. In response to this, companies must design learning programmes that are deeply integrated with the flow of work rather than being seen as a separate, sometimes burdensome, activity.

It's critical, then, to embed learning into the fabric of everyday activities. With sophisticated learning management systems and AI, personalised learning paths can be created, enabling employees to pick up new knowledge and skills in the context of their current projects. As such, learning becomes an ongoing process rather than a discrete event.

Further, the concept of career ladders is becoming outdated. Instead, career 'lattices' offer a more appropriate metaphor for the modern workplace, with employees moving side-to-side, diagonally, and upwards, picking up diverse experiences as they go. Organizations must support this multi-directional growth by acknowledging alternative career paths and providing resources that support a more fluid approach to career development.

In this vein, mentorship takes on a new importance. Seasoned professionals can offer invaluable guidance, facilitating the transfer of tacit knowledge that isn't captured in manuals or traditional training modules. Here cross-generational relationships become strategic assets, blending the expertise of different cohorts to mutual benefit.

Certainly, a culture that rewards risk-taking and experimentation is also pivotal. Institutions must create safe-to-fail environments where employees feel encouraged to apply their learning in innovative ways. Celebrating both successes and constructive failures fosters a growth-oriented mindset that is indispensable in an era of continuous change.

Ultimately, organizations must also recognise the role of autonomy in learning. The Alpha Generation, following in the footsteps of Gen Z, will crave the independence to learn in ways that suit their individual styles. Employers, therefore, should not just provide the resources but also empower their workforce to take charge of their own professional development.

All this pivots on the greater goal of aligning individual aspirations with organisational objectives. A learning ecosystem that is symbiotic, catering to the growth of both the employee and the enterprise, is one that will thrive amid the accelerating cycles of innovation and disruption.

Moreover, external partnerships with academic institutions, online platforms, and industry bodies can enrich the learning ecosystem. They bring fresh insights, resources, and opportunities for employees to gain certifications and formal qualifications that both elevate their own profiles and enhance the company's intellectual capital.

Incentivising learning is another aspect to be tackled with care. By integrating professional growth with performance assessments and progression opportunities, companies embed a natural incentive for employees to keep learning. This could look like recognising employees who upskill with badges, awards, or even compensation adjustments.

Integrating all of these facets requires strategic forethought and deliberate action. Continuous adaptation and lifelong learning are no longer optional perks but foundational elements of a robust talent management strategy. As leaders, HR professionals, and strategists, the charge is clear – to nurture an environment that values perpetual growth, and in doing so, craft organizations that are resilient, agile, and prepared for the generations that lie in wait.

As we stand at the cusp of welcoming the Alpha Generation, we're not just looking to 'future-proof' our workplaces, but to 'future-embrace' them; to create a world of work that flourishes on the very notion of evolution, and where continuous learning and adaptation are ingrained into the very ethos of our professional lives.

Conclusion

The journey towards integrating Generation Z into the fabric of our workforce is indeed an intricate one, marked by shifts in technology, societal values, and global interactions. We have delved deep into the identity of Gen Z, unraveling their ethos, dissecting their technological prowess, and unraveling the new paradigms of leadership and collaboration that resonate with them. As we stand at the precipice of change, it's clear that the inclusion of this dynamic cohort is not just advantageous but imperative for future-ready businesses.

The insights gleaned throughout our discourse point to an undeniable truth: Generation Z's entry into our offices and industries brings with it winds of change. Their digital nativity, a keenness for innovation, and a potent mix of entrepreneurial spirit and socio-environmental consciousness offer a multifaceted lens through which traditional business models are being reconsidered and redefined.

In crafting workplaces that are not just appealing but conducive to the flourishing of Gen Z talent, we've understood the importance of designing agile, collaborative spaces. We've recognised the necessity of flexible hierarchies, the power of mentorship, and the potential of technologies that permit seamless integration of remote and physical realities.

Our strategies for recruitment, engagement, and communication have been thoroughly vetted to fit the unique profile of Generation Z. From leveraging the omnipresent realm of social media to understanding the nuances of their aspirational goals, we've equipped ourselves with a compass to navigate the terrains of a new generational workforce.

We have also acknowledged that the path forward is lit by the torch of continual learning and evolution, where microlearning, tailored development opportunities, and a culture of feedback hold paramount importance. Indeed, our commitment to the financial, mental, and overall wellbeing of our Gen Z colleagues is not just a matter of compliance but core to the ethos of modern leadership.

The pursuit of diversity, inclusivity, and empowerment has emerged as a cornerstone, with these values deeply enshrined in the ways we recruit, progress, and nurture the talent of tomorrow. And as we embrace the technological and legal frameworks that protect and enable Gen Z, we've also aimed to champion their entrepreneurial and intrapreneurial spirit within our corporate arenas.

Performance management, a once static and inflexible process, has undergone its own revolution. The introduction of continuous feedback mechanisms and real-time analytics has transformed how we view, assess, and encourage the potential within our teams.

We've seen the value in extending our vision beyond the office walls, turning our Gen Z employees into genuine brand advocates and harnessing the power of their authenticity in our storytelling and marketing initiatives. They have taught us that a brand's narrative is more compelling when its protagonists truly embody the story's values.

Furthermore, in stepping onto the global stage, we've emphasised cultural intelligence and sensitivity – appreciating that the Gen Z workforce is not monolithic but beautifully diverse, with nuances that traverse nationalities and geographies.

Sustainability has been brought to the forefront as a competitive advantage, influencing not just operational practices but also corporate identity. Generation Z has become a significant catalyst for businesses to constructively measure their impact on people, the planet, and profit, fostering transparency and accountability.

Anticipating the future of work, our projections have been heavily influenced by the predilections of Generation Z, whose values point us towards careers marked by flexibility, autonomy, and purpose. This foresight demands that we stay vigilant and adaptable, not only embracing change but becoming its champions.

The challenges of resistance to change, while formidable, have been dissected to derive methods of ensuring smooth transitions and organizational resilience. In charting this course, we've also honoured the success stories and pioneering companies that have opened the gates and lit the torch for others to follow.

And, with our sights set firmly on embracing continuous adaptation and lifelong learning, we are preparing not just for the now but for the future iterations of our workforce. Looking beyond Generation Z, we're laying the groundwork for the onboarding of the Alpha Generation who will soon follow.

In summary, the integration of Generation Z into the workplace is an ongoing masterpiece, painted with broad strokes of thoughtful innovation, inclusion, resilience, and adaptability. It challenges our norms, inspires our growth, and, most importantly, enriches our collective human experience within the modern business landscape.

As forward-thinking executives, HR leaders, and organizational strategists, our task is thus an exciting and pivotal one. For in supporting Generation Z today, we are not merely investing in the workforce of tomorrow but sculpting a vibrant and sustainable future that we can proudly hand over to the enterprising minds that will soon become the backbone of our society. Let's continue to lead, adapt, and flourish together, as we shape the world through the fresh perspectives and boundless potential that Generation Z brings to our collective table.

Appendix A:
Appendix

After delving into the multifaceted world of Generation Z and strategising for the vibrancy and ingenuity they bring to our work environments, it's clear that continuous learning is the key to staying ahead. This appendix is your gateway to an array of resources that complement the strategies and insights shared throughout our exploration. It's curated with an eye toward the executive, HR leader, or strategist who's not just leading a team, but shaping a progressive workplace.

Additional Resources for Leaders

Empowerment stems from knowledge. As such, our resource list isn't just a compendium of further reading, it's a toolkit for leaders to shepherd their organizations into a future where Gen Z's potential shines brightest.

Industry Reports and Whitepapers: Authored by leading think tanks and research organisations, these documents offer high-level insights into emerging industry trends, the latest in technological adoption, and the evolving expectations of the Gen Z workforce.

Online Learning Platforms: Websites offering courses on a host of topics relevant to leadership, diversity, and technology provide a flexible approach to professional development that resonates with the learning habits of Generation Z.

Case Study Repositories: Real-world examples of companies that have successfully integrated Gen Z into their ranks, showing how theory translates into practice. These narratives showcase not only the successes but also the challenges overcome on the road to organisational harmony.

Policy Framework Templates: As the legal landscape continues to evolve, these templates offer a starting point for ensuring the policies crafted at your organisation are inclusive, up-to-date, and Gen Z-friendly.

Communication Toolkits: Essential for bridging the gap between generations, these toolkits aid in tailoring messaging to the strengths and preferences of a diverse workforce, facilitating collaboration and nurturing a culture of inclusiveness.

Mentorship Program Guides: Step-by-step instructions for setting up mentorship programs that appeal to Gen Z's desire for growth, learning, and connection with seasoned professionals.

Wellbeing Initiatives: Programs and plans that highlight the importance of mental health and wellbeing, reflecting the values held dear by Gen Z and crucial for their productivity and job satisfaction.

Sustainability Roadmaps: Strategies for integrating eco-friendly practices into everyday business operations, designed to resonate with Generation Z's strong sentiment towards environmental concerns.

In the age where information is ever-flowing and change is the only constant, these resources are meant to be your companions, evolving alongside your leadership journey. Prioritise them, adapt them to your organisation's culture, and use them as a springboard for dialogue with Gen Z employees, who are as much a part of tomorrow's solutions as they are a reflection of today's priorities.

Forge ahead with confidence, knowing you're equipped with an understanding of Gen Z and the tools to create an environment where innovation, inclusivity, and growth are not merely welcomed but are the cornerstone of your organisational ethos.

Additional Resources for Leaders

In the ever-evolving business landscape, leaders are racing not just to keep pace but to stay ahead of the curve. Welcome to "Additional Resources for Leaders," a curated collection within the Appendix that serves as an invaluable toolkit for executives, HR professionals, and organisational strategists. Designed to supplement the insights gained from the previous chapters, this section provides a multitude of resources tailored for streamlining the integration of Generation Z into the workforce.

The journey of melding different generations under one corporate roof is nuanced. As you've discovered, the dynamics that Gen Z brings to the table are unique, and embracing these can vault your organisation to new heights. Whether it's about fostering innovation, embracing inclusivity, or setting the stage for future-ready business environments, the resources listed here are your compass in the uncharted terrain of modern workforce management.

First and foremost, we have a selection of cutting-edge scholarly articles that delve deeper into generational psychology and the latest social science research. These explore the intricate motivations and behaviours of Gen Z, adding depth to the understanding you've developed through the initial chapters of this book. These articles serve as a bedrock for formulating evidence-based strategies that resonate with this dynamic cohort.

Additionally, we offer access to exclusive webinars featuring thought leaders and industry stalwarts who have pioneered the integration of Gen Z into their companies. Their firsthand experiences, case studies, and Q&A sessions provide rich, real-world insights that are not found in traditional academic literature. It's practical wisdom, served straight from the trenches of organisational transformation.

Leaders will also find comprehensive guides on utilising technological tools that cater to Gen Z's digital fluency. From collaborative platforms to learning management systems, these resources are tailored for leaders to deploy technology that not only enhances productivity but also appeals to the tech-savvy inclinations of this generation.

Fostering innovation is a collective pursuit, and to that end, we offer resources that assist in building incubator programmes and innovation labs. These are spaces where the entrepreneurial spirit of Gen Z can thrive, and where their fresh perspectives can be harnessed to drive your business forward.

Within this treasure trove, you'll also discover podcasts that cover a range of pertinent topics, including diversity, inclusivity, and the future of work. These episodes are easily digestible, offering busy leaders the flexibility to engage with content during their commutes or between meetings, keeping the thread of continuous learning alive.

A vital inclusion to our resources is a compilation of best practices for mental health management and work-life integration. Here, leaders will gain access to frameworks that underline the importance of these domains and how to effectively support Gen Z's well-being in the workplace.

In the realm of development and training, our repository includes workshops and modular courses designed to appeal to Gen Z's learning preferences. Emphasising microlearning and tailored development plans, these resources are key in crafting a learning ecosystem that resonates with the aspirations of younger employees.

Moving beyond theoretical frameworks, we have detailed templates for implementing mentorship programmes that pair experienced professionals with Gen Z protégés. This intergenerational exchange is not just about knowledge transfer, but also about fostering a culture of mutual respect and collaborative growth.

For leaders seeking to refine their recruitment strategies, our resources include creative recruitment campaign examples, tips on leveraging social media, and insights into Gen Z's job-seeking behaviours. This is imperative for attracting top-tier Gen Z talent that aligns with your organisational goals and values.

On the more practical side of day-to-day operations, a selection of policy templates and compliance checklists will assist in the seamless transition to Gen Z-friendly policies. Covering everything from cybersecurity to diversity initiatives, these resources ensure leaders remain on the right side of change, as well as the law.

No resource page would be complete without a series of links to online forums and professional networks where leaders can engage with peers, share experiences, and seek advice. These vibrant communities are hotbeds of collective knowledge, offering support and shared learning that go beyond conventional wisdom.

The remaining resources invite you into the academic realm, with recommended courses and certifications for leaders eager to polish their management skills for a new generation. These are thoughtfully curated to bolster your expertise in areas directly relevant to leading a Gen Z workforce.

Lastly, with an eye on the future, you'll find subscriptions to publications and trend reports that monitor the pulse of emerging workplace trends. Staying informed about the trajectories of the modern workforce gives leaders the foresight needed to navigate a landscape that Gen Z is rapidly reshaping.

This section of the Appendix is more than a mere supplement; it's a springboard for leaders to leap into action, armed with knowledge and fortified with the tools necessary to not only comprehend but also capitalise on the unique strengths and needs of Generation Z. As the torchbearers of progress within your organisations, leveraging these additional resources is not just an option— it's a strategic imperative for cultivating a thriving, future-proof business.

Glossary of Key Terms

In the swiftly evolving workplace, clarity is key. This glossary equips you with concise definitions for recurrent terms within this book that are crucial for understanding and engaging Generation Z. As we navigate through the intricacies of integrating this dynamic cohort into contemporary business environments, let's ensure we're aligned on terminology.

A

Agile Environments - Workspaces or processes designed to be flexible, fast-responding, and adaptable. Often related to iterative project management and software development, this term has found broader applicability in creating work cultures that can pivot quickly to change.

Authenticity - The practice of being genuine and transparent in one's actions and communication, particularly resonant with Gen Z, who tend to favour brands and employers that uphold this value.

Aspirational Goals - Ambitions or targets that reflect higher aims or ideals, especially those of Gen Z, who are often driven by values and purpose in their career choices.

B

Brand Advocates - Individuals, often employees, who promote and support the brand they are associated with, driving authenticity and peer influence in ways that resonate powerfully with Gen Z consumers and talent.

Belonging - The feeling of security and support when there is a sense of acceptance, inclusion, and identity for a member of a certain group or workplace.

C

Cultural Intelligence - The capability to relate and work effectively across cultures, quintessential in today's globalised business landscape and particularly in engaging with the culturally cognisant Gen Z.

Cybersecurity - The practice of protecting systems, networks, and programs from digital attacks. For Gen Z, who are digital natives, this is an area of concern and expertise.

Collaborative Growth - A development approach that emphasizes teamwork, mentorship, and shared learning experiences, aligning with Gen Z's preference for collective progress and innovation.

D

Digital Natives - Individuals born or brought up during the age of digital technology and thus are familiar with computers and the Internet from an early age. Gen Z is often described as the most seamless adopters of digital innovation.

Diversity - The inclusion of individuals with different characteristics and backgrounds, such as race, ethnicity, gender, sexual orientation, and socioeconomic status. Diversity is not just a value but a strategic advantage when engaging with Gen Z talent.

E

Ethical Business Practices - Actions by companies that are morally right, honourable, and responsible. Ethical practices are a priority for Gen Z, who tend to favour companies that demonstrate social responsibility.

Emotional Intelligence - The capacity to be aware of, control, and express one's emotions judiciously and empathetically. Emotional intelligence is crucial in today's workplace, especially for managing the mental health and wellbeing of Gen Z staff.

Eco-Friendly Practices - Sustainable and environmentally responsible methods of operation that minimize ecological impact, which Gen Z employees and consumers increasingly demand from businesses.

F

Flexibility - The quality of bending without breaking, essential for modern business models, especially as they adapt to Gen Z's preference for adaptable work schedules, locations, and roles.

G

Gamification - The application of game design elements in non-game contexts to improve user engagement, motivation, and loyalty. It's a strategic approach to motivation that has shown efficacy with Gen Z employees and customers.

Generation Z (Gen Z) - The demographic cohort following the Millennials, typically defined as those born from the mid-1990s to mid-2000s. This cohort is at the centre of this book's discourse.

I

Inclusivity - The practice or policy of providing equal access to opportunities and resources for all, particularly those who might otherwise be excluded. Inclusivity in the workplace fosters engagement, innovation, and loyalty among Gen Z employees.

Intrapreneurship - The practice of developing innovative projects within a company, embodying the entrepreneurial spirit among employee ranks, which aligns well with Gen Z's ambition and creativity.

M

Microlearning - A holistic approach to skill-based learning and education where learners study in small, manageable units. This method is particularly appealing and effective for Gen Z workers.

Mentorship - A development relationship in which a more experienced or more knowledgeable person helps to guide a less experienced or knowledgeable person, a practice highly acclaimed and desired by Gen Z employees.

P

Privacy Concerns - Apprehensions regarding the safeguarding of personal information, which are heightened among Gen Z given their digital fluency and the prevalence of data breaches in the modern age.

Performance Management - The process of ensuring that an organization's resources are being properly managed in a way that meets the company's goals, today revolutionised by continual feedback mechanisms, an approach popular with the Gen Z workforce.

R

Remote Work Arrangements - The practice of employees working from a location other than a central office, favoured by Gen Z for its provision of a flexible and autonomy-driven work environment.

S

Social Responsibility - The obligation of individuals or organizations to act for the benefit of society at large. For Gen Z, this is a non-negotiable aspect of any business they associate with as employees or consumers.

Sustainability - The ability to maintain certain processes or states indefinitely. In business, it refers to eco-friendly practices and economic strategies that conserve resources for future generations – a critical concern for Gen Z.

Understanding these terms is pivotal for harnessing the strengths and addressing the nuances of integrating Gen Z into your workforce. This vocabulary serves as the bedrock for strategies that promote innovation, inclusivity, and sustainability – principles that are no longer optional but the cornerstones of a prosperous, future-ready business.